GOALS
TAKE
YOU TO
THE TOP!

Also by Zig Ziglar

Master Successful Personal Habits

The Secrets of Successful Selling Habits

GOALS TAKE YOU TO THE TOP!

How to Get What You Want

Zig Ziglar

MEDIA

Published 2023 by Gildan Media LLC
aka G&D Media
www.GandDmedia.com

Front cover design by David Rheinhardt of Pyrographx

Design by Meghan Day Healey of Story Horse, LLC

Library of Congress Cataloging-in-Publication Data is available upon request

ISBN: 978-1-7225-0645-2

10 9 8 7 6 5 4 3 2 1

Contents

Introduction

"If you aim at nothing
you will hit it every time!"
—Zig Ziglar

Chances are really good that you have this book because you are aiming at something. Congratulations! You have taken the first step in consistently achieving goals and that is to choose to aim at something. This book is going to give you three very specific benefits on your journey to The Top.

1. You are going to get clarity like you have never had before on what your goals are. The clearer the vision of the target you have, the more likely you are to hit the bullseye.

2. You will learn to identify every aspect of the plan you need to create and execute in order to hit the bullseye of every goal you set.

3. You will be empowered to reignite your belief and your desire to hit your goals when life gets in the way. Keep this book handy; read it and listen to it regularly.

Bonus Pro Tip—a powerful way to learn is to have the hard copy in your hand, pen at the ready, while you are also listening to the book on audio. Something magical happens when you hear, see, and write at the same time.

You are on your way to The Top! When you get there, just remember what Dad said, "There is plenty of room at the top, just not enough to sit down."

Tom Ziglar,
CEO Zig Ziglar Corporation

Chapter 1
Your Goals Program

In 1920, Stanford University embarked on a study of 1,440 genius-level youngsters. They followed them all of their life. When the man who originally did the research retired, they simply passed it on in his department. Here's what they discovered. Those who became outstanding successes were not successful because of their genius. They were successful because they had the ability to focus on what was important and persist until they reached it.

Now you don't have to be a genius to do that. Let me simply encourage you to take seriously the messages I'm about to give you, because if you do, I will see you—and yes, I really do mean *you*—at the top.

In this chapter, I'm going to be talking about the complete goals program. Lots of people have individual goals, but very few people have goals programs.

Once I was up in the Pacific Northwest, not far from Portland, Oregon, and I was speaking to the Northwestern Lumbermen's Association. Those lumbermen were big dudes; they all looked as if they could have been playing defensive end for the Dallas Cowboys. The man in charge had told me, "Zig, these people like to hear a lot of stories and jokes, so be sure to tell those."

I was going full speed ahead when all of a sudden, a great big dude about six feet four, who weighed about 275 pounds, stood up and said, "Zig, I have a story I want to tell you."

Well, I have a standard policy. If anybody who's six feet four and weighs 275 pounds wants to tell me a story, I let them. So I said, "Go ahead, partner."

He said, "I want to tell you about my buddy, Bill. Stand up, Bill." A little dude about five feet two inches tall, who couldn't have weighed over 120 pounds soaking wet, stood up. The big guy said, "This is my buddy, Bill Carlotta. Old Bill had come into camp here a few weeks ago, walked up to me, and said, 'Shake hands with your new tree topper.'

"I looked at him, and I said, 'Bill, a tree topper? That's the dude that climbs all the way to the top of the tree and cuts the top out, and then has to hang on for dear life. Bill, that's a job for a man, and you're just a boy.'

"Old Bill pulled off his shirt and said, 'I'm a man.' Zig, I'm here to tell you he is a man. He is all muscle. I still wasn't convinced. Old Bill said, 'Tell you what. Let's go out in the woods, pick out a tree, tell me how long it would take your best man to put it on the ground, and I'll do it in half the time.'

"We went out in the woods, and we picked out this spruce tree, and Zig, I don't have a man in camp that could have put it on the ground in less than forty minutes, but old Bill went to work on that sucker, and I'll tell you that ax moved so fast that it looked like a solid sheet. In less then ten minutes, that tree was on the ground.

"I said to him, 'Bill, where on earth did you learn how to cut down trees like that?'

"He said, 'I learned in the Sahara Forest.'

"'In the Sahara Forest? Bill, the Sahara is a desert.'

"He said, 'It is now.'"

Now I think you'll agree that that guy had a positive attitude, like the lady who was being treated by her hairdresser to a free beauty treatment on her hundredth birthday. As they were talking, the hairdresser said, "You know, you are exactly twice as old as I am." Then it got awfully quiet, and the lady getting the permanent looked terribly depressed.

"What's the matter?" asked the hairdresser.

"I was just thinking. Who on earth am I going to get to take care of my hair when you get too old to do it?"

That lady too was an optimistic person.

A lot of people go prepared. I heard about this fellow who was the speaker at a banquet. For the dinner that evening, there was a Greek salad, and there was an olive pit in it. As you know, olive pits are terrifically hard. They're like rocks. He bit down on it and broke his denture plate.

He was very distressed, and he said to the guy next to him, "I don't know what I'm going to do. My plate is broken."

The guy said, "That's no problem." He reached in his pocket and pulled out a plate. "See if this will fit."

The first man slipped it on and said, "No, it's too big."

"No problem," said the other man. He reached in another pocket and pulled out another one.

The first guy put it in and said, "No, this one's too little."

His companion reached into yet a third pocket, pulled out another one.

"Perfect fit," said the first guy. "Man, how lucky can you get? Here I am breaking my plate, and I sit down next to a dentist."

"I'm not a dentist," said the second guy. "I'm an undertaker." Now there was someone who was prepared.

The Cafeteria Plan

As we look at a goals program, life is very much like a cafeteria line. A number of years ago the redhead (as I lovingly refer to my wife at her request) and I saw this new cafeteria. We knew it was going to be good, because the line was always out the door.

We weren't willing to wait that long in line, so we kept going past. Then one day we rode past, and we couldn't see a line, so I said, "Hey, it looks like we can get in there today. Let's go." We parked and walked in, and we understood why the line was not outside, because it was wound all over inside the building.

We'd already parked, so we got in line with around thirty people, and as we got down to the end of the line, we turned around and saw another line of thirty people. Eventually we could see the food.

As we walked down the line, I said to myself, "Now, I'm going to get me some of that, and I want me some of that. That looks good. I'll have me some of that. I want some of that." I love to eat in cafeterias. I like to see what I'm going to eat before I choose it. So I'd already made up my mind. That's important, because I don't care how prodigious your appetite is: you cannot eat some of everything that's on the line.

I didn't delay anybody. I knew what I wanted. I got to the end of the line, reached in, and took out my money. The lady at the end of the line held up her hand and said, "No. You don't pay for it until you get ready to leave."

"You mean you're going to let me eat all this food before I pay for it?"

"Yes, that's just the way we do it."

I have thought about that a lot of times. Life is exactly like a cafeteria inasmuch as we have so many things to choose from. In that particular line, you get to eat, and then you pay. Life is not like that line inasmuch as in life, you pay and then you eat.

Your employer will make you work from two to four weeks before he or she will give you a dime. That's the way we treat our people. We make them work before we give them the pay.

The farmer plants the crop, raises it, fertilizes it, and harvests it. Then and only then can it go to the marketplace, and he'll be rewarded for his effort.

Students study their lessons. Then they take the test. Then they graduate. Then they receive their reward.

The point is very simple. You have to do those things before you're rewarded.

The farmer plants the crop, raises it, fertilizes it, and harvests it. Then and only then can it go to the marketplace, and he'll be rewarded for his effort.

What Everyone Wants

Now let's identify what everybody wants. Everyone wants to be happy. They want to be healthy. They want to be to be at least reasonably prosperous. They want to be secure. They want to have friends. They want to have peace of mind. They want to have good family relationships, and by all means, they want to have hope.

If you want those things, specifically identify all of them as goals and write them down.

Next, list all the benefits. That's very important. A lot of people talk only about the problems: "I'd go back to school and get my degree, but it'd take me ten years. By then I'll be forty-five years old." But how old will you be in ten years if you *don't* get your degree?

We concentrate on the obstacles and the difficulties instead of the benefits. If a salesperson only talked about the price, how much would they sell? Instead, they talk about the benefits that come with the product. Somebody who has braces on their teeth isn't happy while they're wearing them, but they're wearing them for the benefits that come later. So list the benefits.

Do you have the necessary skills and knowledge to reach this objective? Identify the obstacles. There are obstacles in life; we have to identify them.

You also have to identify the individuals, groups, and organizations to work with. You have to develop a plan of action, with a completion date. That's what goal planning is really all about.

Tips for goal achievement

- Identify your wants, set your goals and write them down.
- List the benefits you will get from achieving the goals.
- Identify the obstacles to your goals (Do you have enough skill and knowledge to achieve it?)
- Make a plan of action (identify the individuals, groups and organizations to work with)
- Set a completion date.

Happiness Is Victory

Now a question may come up: "Wait a minute, Ziglar. You said that everybody wants to be happy. Can you really set happiness as a goal?"

All of my life, I've been told that you can't set happiness as a goal, but let's explore this question. Happiness, like money, is the result of what you do. Let's look at the qualities of success. If you were honest, hardworking, enthusiastic, dependable, and responsible, how would you feel about yourself? The image you would have of yourself would be good.

If you're happy with yourself, if you know that you're using the ability you have, your chances of being happy dramatically improve. Happiness is not a *when* or a *where*. It is a *here* and a *now*.

A lot of people think they'll be happy when they get a new home. Then they think they'll be happy when they get everything arranged properly in it. Then they'll be happy when they get the new furniture. Then they'll be happy when they finish paying for it. Then they think they'll be happy when they get the patio and the backyard landscaping done.

For these people, happiness is always a when or where: "I'll be happy when I win the trip to Hawaii. I'll be happy when I get there." No, you will not be happy in a when or where.

Happiness is not a *when* or a *where*. It's a *here* and a *now*.

You may have fun in Hawaii, but I love what Dennis Prager said in a *Reader's Digest* article: "Fun is what we experience during an act. Happiness is what we experience after an act. It is a deeper, more abiding emotion." He says that things like going to an amusement park or ball game, watching a movie or television, or other fun activities help us to temporarily forget our problems and maybe even laugh, but they do not bring happiness, because their positive effect ends when the fun ends. Happiness is of a much longer duration.

Mr. Prager also points out with unusual insight that the belief that a fun-filled, pain-free life equals happiness actually diminishes people's chances of ever attaining real happiness. If fun and play are equated with happiness, then pain must be equated with unhappiness, but in fact the opposite is true. More times than not, things that lead to happiness involve some pain.

Happiness is not pleasure. It's victory—victory over things that are tough, victory over odds that sometimes seem to be insurmountable.

We also have to understand that you can lose what you have and still be what you are. That's very important, because if you're what you are, if that's what you build on, your chances of being happy increase substantially.

Let's take another look at this question. You may believe that if your health is good, if you're reasonably prosperous, if you're secure within yourself and what you do, if you have friends, peace of mind, and good family relationships, and if you have hope for the future, your chances of happiness would be much improved.

We can set every one of these as objectives. As you reach the objective of having friends, peace of mind, and better family relationships, won't that definitely contribute to your happiness?

Of course. (I'll help you with the tough ones.) There is no doubt about it.

I'm convinced that peace of mind comes from resolving the question of what happens to us when we die; in other words, where will we spend eternity? That has a direct bearing on happiness.

If you have all of these things, it definitely improves your chances of being happy, but let me ask you a question. Do you believe that life is fragile? Have you known somebody who is happy one day and miserable the next?

For example, you can be completely healthy one day, then tragically injured in an accident. If your happiness is only wrapped up in your health, then happiness goes away. That's one reason that we need to understand the difference between a *problem* and a *condition*.

John Foppe is an outstanding man who was born without any arms. Being without arms is not a problem; it is a condition. If he makes a problem out of it, then he will never be happy, because he will never have arms, but if he recognizes it is a condition, then he can learn to deal with it. That's one way he stays optimistic, motivated, and happy.

Being, Doing, and Having

Let me make a very profound statement: you can't always keep what you *have*, but you can keep what you *are*.

Take a sheet of paper and draw three vertical sections on it. At the top of the left one, put "Be"; at the top of the middle one, put "Do"; and at the top of the last one, put "Have." If you list the things in your life that fall into these categories, you will discover that everything you *have* is a result of what you *are* and what you *do*. So that's what we want to work on.

A lot of people get confused about happiness. They think it means they have to be ecstatic all of the time. Let me tell you something: All sunshine makes a desert. If all you ate was ice cream, you would get sick and tired of ice cream.

Many times, our greatest trials and tribulations produce the greatest happiness. I've never yet had a mother describe how much fun she had while giving birth to a child, but I have had many of them say that after the pain was gone, they felt ecstasy, joy, and delight. They say that happiness made them almost

"You can't always keep what you *have*,
but you can keep what you *are*." —Zig Ziglar

immediately forget what they went through during labor.

During labor, a lot of mothers say, "This is going to be the only one of these I will ever have," but then the experience that goes with holding that little one in their hands makes them forget about the trauma of the birth.

Genuine happiness comes from who you are and what you do with who you are. A lot of people get a lot of pleasure—I do—in sinking a forty-foot putt. I was delighted when the Cowboys defeated the Buffalo Bills and won the Super Bowl. I was ecstatic, but let me ask you a question.

Do you really think that every Buffalo Bills fan in America is miserable and unhappy just because the Bills lost the Super Bowl? That doesn't mean they didn't want to win—maybe worse than we did—but it means that that was an event, and their lives are not going to be controlled or determined by that particular event. People who think they can be happy all the times simply are not dealing with the reality of life.

The Ziglar Goal Setting System

This chapter is titled, Your Goals Program, because everyone needs a specific, step-by-step system for achieving the specific goals that will bring them the greatest amount of happiness, success, fulfillment and sense of contribution in their life. While I will spend the majority of this book doing what I do best—

selling you on the importance of goals, inspiring you with anecdotes of others who are models of goal achievement, and motivating you to stay on track with you goals program—I want to introduce you to what I consider to be the greatest goal setting system ever assembled. It's the Ziglar Goal Setting System. At this point, please turn to the Appendix at the very end of the book, where you'll see the 8 Action Steps of the system and worksheets you can use (feel free to make Xerox copies of them for your own use if you like) to customize this system for yourself. I suggest you review the Ziglar Goal Setting System in detail, and even better, go through all of the steps so you can have your own goals in place, prior to continuing on with the chapters that follow. Having your own list of goals in mind will help you to get maximum value from the rest of this book. And having your own goals burned into your mind, will pull you through any roadblock on your journey to success. And we'll cover that topic in our next chapter—Obstacles to Achieving Your Goals.

Chapter 2
Obstacles to Achieving Your Goals

Everybody has goals. For example, you probably have a goal of reading this book. But a heroin addict also has a goal. So does an alcoholic.

There are four reasons why 97 percent of all the people in our society do not have one. The first is fear. *Fear* is an acronym for *False Evidence Appearing Real.*

What do I mean? A young Cuban hijacked a plane to Cuba with a bar of soap. That's all he had. He put the bar of soap in a box and said to the captain, "It's a bomb. Let's go to Cuba." They went to Cuba.

I could take a handkerchief and rob a bank. All I'd have to do is put the handkerchief over my face, put my hand in my pocket, pretend I had a gun in there, and say, "Give me your money." The evidence would be false, but it would appear real, and consequently the bank would be robbed. I might get shot on the way out, but in virtually every case, I would be successful at least in frightening the individual I was dealing with.

A lot of times as youngsters, we are given information about ourselves that is absolutely erroneous. We buy into that idea and carry it with us, in many cases for the rest of our lives.

We need to understand that failure is an event. It is not a person. Yesterday really did end last night. Today is a brand-new day, and it's yours. Regardless of what happened yesterday, you do not need to let it control what you're doing today.

This goes right back to a fact that I mention in every book I write: the image you have of yourself is a determining factor in your attitude in everything else that you do.

A lot of times we accumulate false evidence: for example, that it's dangerous to fly in airplanes. You may have seen pictures of wrecked planes. They're in pretty bad shape. It's dangerous for you to fly, but it's more dangerous for the airplane, because when those suckers come down from thirty thousand feet up, the trade-in value on them is worth hardly anything. You can't swap them in at all.

It is more dangerous, however, for the plane to stay on the ground. Experts will tell you that that plane will rust out faster sitting on the runway than it will wear out flying in the heavens. That's what airplanes are built for.

It's dangerous for a ship to leave the harbor. It might not get back, but it is more dangerous for it to stay in the harbor. The experts again say that it will collect barnacles and deteriorate faster riding at anchor than it will sailing in the high seas, which is what ships are built for.

It is dangerous for you to set goals. You might not get there; you might be embarrassed in front of your friends. But it is infinitely more dangerous not to set the goal.

It's dangerous for a farmer to plant crops. Suppose it rains too much, or not enough. Suppose it gets too cold, or not cold enough. Suppose it's too hot, or not hot enough. It's dangerous to plant those crops, but I think you'll agree that it is infinitely more dangerous for farmers not to plant the crops.

In other words, it is more dangerous not to set goals than it is to set those goals.

I love the way the inspirational pastor Harry Emerson Fosdick said it: "No steam or gas ever drives anything until it is confined. No Niagara is ever turned into light and power until it is tunneled. No life ever grows until it is focused, dedicated, and disciplined."

I absolutely love what Wayne Gretzky, the superstar of hockey, said: "You miss 100 percent of the shots you don't take."

It's more dangerous *not* to set goals, then it is to set goals.

A lot of people fail, not because they don't have the ability, but because they don't recognize that ability and make the effort to be the success they're capable of being.

Self-Image

The second reason 97 percent of people do not have goals has to do with a poor self-image. Change the picture, and you change the performance. Again, you have to be before you can do, and you have to do before you can have.

Psychologist Dr. Joyce Brothers has this to say: "The picture you have of yourself, your self-image, determines the job you seek or profession, the person you marry, the habits you acquire, the way you look and dress, and it influences your moral conduct. You cannot consistently perform in a manner which is inconsistent with the way you see yourself."

There are a lot of people who see themselves as $30,000 a year earners, and when they get there, they can't see beyond that. In golf, we see it happen many times. If someone is a twenty-handicapper, he's shooting in the nineties. He gets out there, and he pars the first hole, he pars the second hole, he birdies the third hole, and he pars the fourth hole. At the end of four holes, there he is—one under par. He starts saying, "Man, I can't believe this. Here I am, one under par after four. Normally at this point, I am about eight over par."

> "You cannot consistently perform in a manner which
> is inconsistent with the way you see yourself."
> —Dr. Joyce Brothers

Guess what happens on the next hole. That's right: a triple bogie: he plays to his handicap. Why? Because he sees himself in that particular light. Change the picture, and you will change the performance.

Self-image is important in every phase of life. Duane Crumb, founder and director of HIV*Hope* International, has this to say: "The foundation for teens to say no to sex is a healthy self-image. It can be summed up in one sentence. Those who say no to sex say, 'I value my future enough to take steps to protect it.'"

The problem of discrimination also dissipates when students believe in themselves. Kids who feel valued are less apt to try to prove themselves by discriminating against others, and they may be motivated to assist those who are different. As the California Task Force to Promote Self-Esteem said, "Persons with healthy self-esteem choose to serve others out of their sense of personal fullness and their joy of being alive. In the process of serving, they deepen and reinforce their own self-esteem."

We can do something about many of our problems, and it centers around a realistic picture of who we are and what we are capable of doing. Self-image is important.

The Story of Tom Hartman

In 1978, I was speaking up in Oklahoma City. It was an all-day seminar. About eighteen months later, I got a letter from a man named Tom Hartman. Since then, I have become a friend of Tom. We've had a number of telephone conversations, personal visits, and much correspondence, and here's the gist of what Tom Hartman had to say about that seminar.

"Zig," he said, "three minutes after I got there, I knew I was in the wrong place. You came out with a lot of enthusiasm and said, 'You can go where you want to go, you can do what you want to do, you can be the way you want to be.'

"I said to myself, I wasn't going to sit there all day long and listen to that kind of baloney. I knew better than that, and I made up my mind that at the first chance, I was going to get out of there, but you kept going, and a few minutes later, you had the gall to say to the audience, 'God loves you.'

"I knew that was a bunch of baloney, and I immediately wanted to leave, but I was right in the middle of sixteen hundred people. I knew that if I left, I was going to create a disturbance, so I said to myself, 'First break, I'm gone, and that will be the end of me and Zig Ziglar.'

"But, Zig, you were such a persistent guy. You kept hammering away. In a few minutes you said, 'You were designed for accomplishment. You're engineered for success. You're endowed with the seeds of greatness.' When you said that, I thought, 'Well, the old boy is finally getting closer to the truth,' because I looked down at myself, and I was looking at a 63½-inch waistline and 406 pounds of bulk.

"I was just coming off a devastating divorce; I hadn't been in a church in years. I had a job only because my boss was my friend—the only friend I had. I wasn't working because I was productive; I was working because, in essence, I was on welfare. My boss was supporting me. I was so broke that on Friday night, I'd go to the grocery store, buy my food, and give them a hot check. Then on Monday morning, when I got my check, I'd rush over to the bank, and I would beat it.

"I was failing in every area of life. I wasn't happy. I wasn't healthy. I wasn't even reasonably prosperous. I certainly did not feel secure. I had only one friend, had no peace of mind, had terrible family relationships, and hope—forget it; in my life, it didn't exist.

"But," he said, "Zig, you kept hammering, and I don't know what it was you said, but you mentioned something, and a lady behind me said, 'That's right.' At that moment, something snapped, and it finally penetrated."

Isn't it interesting? A message can go 24,000 miles around the world in less than a tenth of a second, but sometimes it never penetrates that last quarter of an inch.

"I reached over," said Tom, "I picked up my yellow pad, and I started writing. I wrote fast and furiously all day long. By the end of the day, for the first time in my adult life, I caught just a glimmer of hope. I wanted so desperately to buy a set of your motivational tapes. I didn't have a dime to my name, but my brother, bless his heart, came to the rescue and loaned me the money. I bought the tapes.

"Now, Zig, I listened to you six solid hours that day, then I went home and I listened to you another seven hours. When I got up the next morning, I was a totally different human being. I caught a glimpse of what hope was all about.

"The first thing I did was go to my boss. I said to him with a smile on my face, 'Rest easy. I'm going to start carrying my own weight.' When you weigh 406 pounds, that's a pretty big statement.

"That afternoon, I went over to Oklahoma City University, where I was already taking a couple of courses in history just to have something to do. I switched over to psychology, because I wanted to learn something about my fellow human beings and me.

"That afternoon I went over to the Nautilus health studio to get something done about this miserable body of mine. On Thursday, I went down to the clothing store and laid aside $700 worth of clothes on a mynute down payment. When the owner of the store noticed I was buying size 47 jackets and size 39 slacks, he said, 'Mr. Hartman, who are you getting the clothes for?' When I told him I was getting them for myself, he looked very skeptical, but he said, 'OK.' I knew deep down that he didn't believe for a minute that I was going to be able to lose all of that weight."

Let me make two major points there. One is that Tom Hartman made the commitment and took action immediately. We've discovered that when people first hear this concept of a goals program, if they take action immediately, the chances are at least ten times as high that they'll do something about it. If they delay it, if they say they'll get around to it, you know what happens to that one.

The second major point is that when directions are set and commitments are made, almost immediately help starts showing up all over the place. Let me tell you what I'm talking about.

Tom Hartman said to me, "Zig, I since then have listened to that tape on self-image over five hundred times. I've listened to all of the others a minimum of two hundred times. If you ever develop a sore throat, don't you dare cancel any speaking engagement. Just call me. I can make your talk verbatim. I'll even use your accent.

"Zig, let me tell you what happened. I'm so glad that the police did not observe me as I was listening to those tapes. I'd be riding down the street and I'd be listening to one of your tapes. You'd say, 'You were born to win,' and I'd say, 'Well, how come I'm always losing?' You'd say, 'You can do it,' and I'd say, 'Well, how come I never can or never have?' You'd say, 'Hang in there,' and I'd say, 'Zig, hanging is no fun at all.'

"But, you know, Zig, I noticed something. Sometimes I'd get a little weary, and I didn't have as much enthusiasm when I tried to refute you. But you were always motivated. You were always excited. That recording was always wide open, full-speed ahead, no holds barred. Now, Zig, over a period of time, I came to realize that what you were saying was absolutely right."

There's an old saying that truth can be denied, but it cannot be avoided; ultimately it will get to you. Tom said, "Because you were speaking truth, I believe that if people would just hear it enough times, regardless of how vehemently they might reject it initially, it will penetrate and get through to them, and it will have its impact.

"Zig, I'd been in the program about six weeks. I was in a grocery store buying my food. It was Friday night, and as I was in the store, there was a little four-year-old girl. All of a sudden, I heard a voice screaming loudly enough that you could have heard it from Dallas to Fort Worth. She said, 'Mama, look at that fat man.'

"I whirled around to see where he was. Then, Zig, I realized she was talking about me, and I thought that was the funniest thing I'd ever heard in my life. I got so tickled, I literally laughed until I cried."

Then, he said, "I shed a tear of an entirely different kind, because for the first time in my life, I knew I was going to make it. I knew that I was going to take that weight off and change the other things in my life. The picture had changed."

"About a month later," he said, "I'd been to the movies. I was on my way back to the car. I was in no hurry. I had nothing to do, nowhere to go, nothing to do when I got there. I was just ambling along, and I noticed a display in one of the store windows. I had no interest in the displays." He walked over, he started looking at the display, and he became intrigued with it.

Suddenly, he became aware of the fact that he was not by himself. Some big dude was looking over his shoulder. He whirled around. There was nobody there. He had seen his own reflection, which he did not recognize.

As a good friend of mine, the late Dr. John Kozak, a brilliant young psychiatrist from Dunedin, Florida, said, "At that precise moment, Tom Hartman was no longer obese." Though he still weighed well over 360 pounds, he was no longer obese, because the picture he had of himself had completely changed.

For twenty-four years in my own life, I weighed well over two hundred pounds. I lost tons of weight. It went up and down and up and down, but years ago, when the picture of myself changed, the weight came off. Tom Hartman's picture had changed too.

Now let me emphasize a point. When you start out on a project, you will very quickly discover that there is a conspiracy among people, not to keep you from your objective, but to help you reach it. When you know where you're going, the world gets together

---

When you start out on a project, you will very quickly discover that there is a conspiracy among people, not to keep you from your objective, but to help you reach it.

---

and says, "Here's a lady or here's a man who knows where they're going. I want to go with them, or I want to make it easier for them."

Let me tell you what happened in Tom Hartman's life. Help sometimes comes in a form that appears to be negative but turns out to be positive. One example is the store owner who looked so skeptical and said to himself when Tom bought his clothes, "I don't think he's going to make it." Tom Hartman said, "I will show that dude."

The little girl who said, "Look at the fat man" does not realize how much she helped Tom Hartman in his project. His brother, who bought him those tapes, was certainly an enormous help to him.

I said that Tom listened to that self-image recording over five hundred times. You may say, "You have to be kidding me if you tell me that he benefited over five hundred times every time he listened to it."

Now I'm going to make a very strong statement, which I cannot prove: I honestly believe that more people have lost more weight and kept it off as a direct result of listening to my recordings than of any diet book that you've ever seen.

That's a strong statement. But I've had people by the hundreds start a conversation with me by saying, "I started listening to those tapes, and I lost forty pounds" or two hundred pounds or whatever.

Let me explain why that happens. Certain things activate the brain. For example, exciting music floods the system with endorphins, dopamine, norepinephrine, and some of the other neurotransmitters. Exercise will also really get them going. So will having your team win the Super Bowl.

Every time Tom listened to the recording, it activated in some cases the pituitary, in other cases other parts of the brain. His system was then flooded with those chemicals, and he was energized physiologically. Dopamine and norepinephrine give you the energy, endorphins give you the endurance, and all of those are produced by listening to something exciting and motivating.

The way you activate the brain is through something called serotonin. It generally gets busy about ten in the morning, hours after we've started our day.

How do you activate your brain to jumpstart the serotonin? You can do it one of two ways: do something really nice for somebody else, or listen to something that is truly inspiring.

There's also something in the brain called galanin. Galanin is the bad guy. With the person who is overweight, the galanin devours the dopamine or the norepinephrine, so the more overweight you are, the lower your energy level goes.

Tom Hartman was activating the brain to produce more dopamine, norepinephrine, and endorphins, and as a result, he developed the energy. He was burning fat instead of consuming it.

That's one of the most exciting breakthroughs that I have ever heard of in my life. Again, when the picture you have of yourself changes, then everything in your life is going to change.

Selling You on Your Goals

The third reason that 97 percent of the people do not have a goals program is because they have never been sold. That's my objective now. I'm flat out going to sell you on why you have to have a goals program. I'm not going to *try* to sell you. I'm not going to *hope* to sell you. I am flat out *going* to sell you on why you have to have this program.

The typical person in America is what I call a wandering generality. They go to work tomorrow because that's what they did yesterday. If that's their reason for going to work, they're not going to be any better; in fact they might not be as good as they were yesterday, because now they're two days older, and they still have no specific direction in their lives.

The typical individual on the job thinks, "I ought to be spending more time with my family." When they're spending time with their family, they think, "I ought to be out there working for my family." Their mind is in one place, their body is in another, and then they wonder why they're not more effective.

The exciting thing about a goals program is that it enables you to focus so that you're more effective both at home and on the job. You will then have extra time for growth, for education, for the activities which will make you more productive in life.

J.C. Penney expressed it enormously well a number of years ago when he said, "Give me a man who is a stock clerk who has a goal, and I will give you a man who will make history. You give me a man who is a stock clerk without a goal, and I'll give you a stock clerk." Again, it is not where you are; it's where you go.

"Give me a man who is a stock clerk who has a goal, and I will give you a man who will make history."
—J.C. Penny

The Story of Lou Holtz

One of my favorite stories is about a young coach who was fired from his first coaching job at the University of South Carolina. A new head coach had come in and let the whole staff go, but he liked this young coach and gave him some fatherly advice: "Son, you're not cut out to be a coach. I encourage you to get into some other field."

At that time the young man had a dream: to be the head football coach at the University of Notre Dame. He thanked the man for his advice and decided he would continue to pursue his career. At Ohio State University, Woody Hayes gave him a chance.

Later, William and Mary College made him head coach. He did such a fabulous job there that he got a chance to be head coach at North Carolina State University, where he built the best won/lost record that school had ever experienced.

This young man had a short stay of one year in the pros. He loved to teach young people and ended up as the head coach at the University of Arkansas, where, again, he built the best won/lost record they'd ever had.

One year, the team was invited to the Orange Bowl to play the Oklahoma Sooners. Three of his players were caught with a woman in the room. He investigated the story, verified that it actually had happened, and without any hesitation kicked all three of them off the team.

This was his offense: 90 percent of the scoring and 90 percent of the yards had been gained by those three players. The media speculated that Arkansas should withdraw from the Orange Bowl, because they obviously had no chance against Oklahoma. They were underdogs even before he dismissed those three players.

But the coach decided to take stock of what he did have and not worry about what he had lost. He analyzed the fact that he had the number-one punter in the entire nation, the number-one field goal kicker in the entire nation, and the number-one defense in the entire nation. He had the players verbalize their strengths over and over.

The rest, as they say, is history. It almost was a mismatch. They were an inspired football team. They beat Oklahoma very badly.

Later this coach went to the University of Minnesota, which had a tremendous football program and a winning season. When he signed the agreement with them, he asked for two escape clauses. He said, "Number one, if the powers that be at Notre Dame say to me, 'We want you to coach the team,' and if I have had you in a bowl within three years, I want to be released from my agreement." They agreed to it.

At the end of the second year, Notre Dame called Lou Holtz to be their head football coach.

Goals absolutely do work. Let me emphasize something very significant. The people at Notre Dame wanted Lou to be the coach the day he dismissed those three players from his Arkansas football team. They said, "Here's a man who is more interested in developing character and developing people for life instead of just winning football games."

The powers that be said, "If he's ever available at the time we need a coach, he is our man." Goals built on a solid base absolutely do work.

I'm going to repeat this point, because repetition is the mother of learning. That means it is the father of action, which makes it the architect of accomplishment.

The UCLA School of Medicine did a study on the people who come to my seminars, set goals programs, and develop a plan of action for following through on their programs. Here's what they learned.

Those who set their goals and develop a plan of action earn an average of $7,401 a month. Those who get exactly the same information and think it's nice, but it's not for me, maybe later but not now, earn an average of $3,397 a month. It pays to set goals.

You know what's even more exciting? That study showed, number one, that family life improved for the people who set goals. Number two, their health also improved. Number three, their balance in life itself was infinitely better. That's what a goals program is all about.

You have to have goals. Can you imagine Sir Edmund Hillary, the first man to scale Mount Everest, the tallest mountain in the whole world, climbing down from that mountain and having a reporter ask him, "Tell me, how did you climb the tallest mountain in the whole world? How did you do it?"

Do you think for one moment Hillary said, "Well, I was just out there walking around." Isn't that ridiculous? Yet isn't there an amazing number of people who will spend more time planning the wedding than they will the marriage, who will spend more time planning a two-week vacation than they will their very lives?

As a matter of fact, Edmund Hillary did not scale Mount Everest the first time he tried. He left several of his climbers dead on the mountainside. Even so, the effort was so enormous that the British Parlia-

---

**The benefits derived from those
who follow a goals program**

- They earn more than 2x of those who don't follow a goals program.
- Their family life improved.
- Their health improved.
- Their balance in life was better than those who don't follow a goals program.

—UCLA School of Medicine Study

---

ment called him before them to give him England's highest award. As he walked into that august body, they rose as an individual and gave him a prolonged standing ovation. Up front was a huge picture of the peak of Mount Everest.

Hillary, ignoring the crowd, walked straight to the front of that picture, shook his fist at it, and said, "You won this time, but you're as big as you're ever going to get. I'm still growing."

So you didn't reach your goals the first time you set them. So what? Failure is an event. It is not a person. Yesterday ended last night. Today is a brand-new day. The obstacles might still be there, but when you continue to grow, your chances of scaling them and reaching your goal are dramatically improved.

Can you imagine the chairman of the board for General Motors? Somebody says to him, "How did you get to be the chairman of the board?" He says, "I just showed up for work. They started promoting me, and here I am."

There is no way that happened. We have to have a plan, and the plans that we develop enable us to do far more of the things we really want to do. If you don't have time to set goals now, you probably never have, and you never will.

I don't know how many of you recognize the name of Howard Hill. A good Alabama boy, he entered 283 archery tournaments in his lifetime, and he placed first in all 283. He killed a Cape buffalo and a Bengal tiger with a bow and arrow. I have seen him in newsreels hit the bull's-eye dead center from fifty feet away, and then, with his next arrow, split the first one.

Hill was remarkable. They say he could outshoot any rifleman in the world from fifty feet. He killed a fifteen-foot shark in eighteen feet of water—or was it an eighteen-foot shark in fifteen feet of water? Well, all I know is it was big, and it was way down there. He killed it with a bow and arrow.

I've never shot the bow and arrow professionally, but I am an absolutely superb instructor. As a matter of fact, casting modesty aside, I'm going to tell you without any fear of error that I can take any one of you, and if your health is good and your eyesight is good, I could spend twenty minutes with you, and I could have you hitting the bull's-eye more consistently than Howard Hill could have hit it the best day he ever had—provided, of course, we first blindfolded Howard Hill and turned him around a few times so he would have no idea of which direction he was heading in.

You laugh and say, "Why, Ziglar, that's the silliest example I have ever heard in my life. How on earth could a man possibly hit a target he could not even see?"

That's a good question. Here's one, though, that's even better. How can you hit a target you don't even have? Do you have a target?

My objective in all of this is to help you move from survival to stability, from stability to success, and from success to significance.

Now let me ask you again. Did you write your goals down? Did you identify the benefits that would come your way by reaching them? Did you spell out the obstacles you have to climb in order to get there? Did you identify the people, the groups, and the organizations you need to work with in order to get there? Did you develop a plan of action? Did you identify what you need to know? Have you set a date on when you'll get there? That's what I am really talking about when I really get into the goals program.

"I Don't Know How"

A lot of times people say, "OK, Ziglar, the first reason I don't have goals is because of fear. The second reason I don't have goals is because of my poor self-image. The third reason I don't have a goals program is simply that I've never been totally convinced that I have to have them, and the fourth reason that I do not have goals is because I don't know how."

The fourth reason 97 percent of the people don't have goals is they do not know how to put together a goals program. That is the subject of the next chapter.

The reasons people do not set goals

• Fear
• Poor self-image
• Have never been convinced of their importance.
• They don't know how to set up a goals program.

Chapter 3

How to Set Goals

Personally, I think everybody, even sixth-, seventh-, and eighth-graders, ought to write a book entitled *What You Ought to Do to Get the Most Out of Life*. When I wrote my book *See You at the Top*, I could well have put that as the title, because that was really what it was about.

Actually, the first words I wrote in *See You at the Top* were the words I used in the Tom Hartman story earlier: You can go where you want to go. You can do what you want to do. You can be the way you want to be. Those are not the first words in the book, but that's what I had originally written, and as I wrote them, I looked at them and started talking to myself. Now talking to yourself is OK, as I mentioned earlier. Dr. Joyce Brothers says people who talk to themselves

---

"You can go where you want to go. You can do what
you want to do. You can be the way you want to be."
—Zig Ziglar

---

are above average in intelligence, so if you've been
guilty of that, go right ahead.

When I wrote those words, I noticed I was holding the book way out there, because a forty-one-
inch waistline and over two hundred pounds of
Ziglar stood between me and the book. The thought
occurred to me that one day one of you folks would
come up to me, smile, and say, "Ziglar, you believe all
that stuff you write?"

I was going to say, "Of course I do."

Then I could imagine you saying, "Do you believe
it all?"

"Why, certainly I do."

Then I could imagine you poking your finger in
that forty-one-inch waistline and saying, "Ziglar, do
you believe it all?"

Then I would have to say, "Well, you know, we
authors do take a little literary license every once in
a while."

"In other words, Ziglar, you lied."

"Hey, friend, don't call me a liar. People don't like
liars."

"Well, you're at least a hypocrite."

"Don't call me a hypocrite. People sure don't like
hypocrites. Some people don't even go to church

because there's nothing but a bunch of hypocrites down there." (I'm always telling friends, don't let that stop you. Come on down, we have room for one more.)

Anyway, I knew that if I was going to put those words in that book, I had to do something about *me*. So I went to down to the Cooper Clinic, where they put me on a diet and exercise program. Dr. Randy Martin was the examining physician, one of those highly motivated, dedicated, committed, really healthy enthusiasts. He was slender. He was running the Boston Marathon.

The first thing they did was take two quarts of my blood. Well, it looked like two quarts. They filled so many vials I thought they were making a collection for the blood bank; I really did.

Then they put me on the treadmill. You walk and walk, and the longer you can walk, the better your physical condition is.

I looked at that needle, and the worst possible condition was "horrible." I determined to get out of that into just "awful," and I made it by about four seconds. When it was all over, Dr. Martin called me in for the consultation, and he said, "Mr. Ziglar, you're going to be delighted to know that you, sir, are not overweight."

"That is wonderful," I said.

"However, I have to tell you that you are exactly five and one-eighth inches too short."

"Well, doc, what can I do about it?"

He proceeded to give me a thick sheaf of paper, and by the time he'd gotten through, he had told me a whole lot more than I really wanted to know. He ended by saying, "Mr. Ziglar, I just want you to do know that you're in marvelous physical condition."

"That's marvelous."

"For a sixty-six-year-old."

"Doc, I'm forty-six."

He said, "You are in awful shape. I'm telling you it's your perspective," and again, he went through all the things I could do.

When I got home, the redhead said, "I suppose you're going to be out running all over the neighborhood."

"Yes, I am."

"Well, if I'm going to have a forty-six-year-old fat boy running all over the neighborhood, I'm going to get you looking as good as I can," so she went down and bought me some fancy running shirts and shorts; I'd already gotten the shoes the doctor had recommended.

I'd also done did something that was very, very ugly, but I had not read Ann Landers at the time, and I'll use that as my excuse. Ann Landers said you should not steal pages out of other folks' magazines. There was an old magazine in the doctor's office, which had an advertisement for Jockey shorts.

If you've seen Jockey ads, you know they don't put their shorts on fat boys. I took that picture and hung it up on my bathroom mirror. I said, "That's my hero. That's the way I'm going to look right there."

The next morning, the opportunity clock (negative people call them alarm clocks) sounded off at 5:30. I rolled out of bed, put my fancy running outfit on, hit the front door, and ran a block.

But I did better the next day. I ran a block and a mailbox. The next day it was a block and two, and then a block and three, and a block and four, and a block and five. I well remember the day I ran all the way around one block. I woke the whole family up and said, "Guess what Dad has done."

Then, one day, I ran a half a mile, then a mile, then two, then three, then four, then five. I started doing sit-ups. I could only do eight the first time, then ten, then twenty, then thirty, then fifty, then a hundred, then two hundred. I started doing push-ups. I could only do six the first time, then eight, then ten, then twenty, then thirty, then forty.

Later I was able to do the GI push-up: you push up, and while you're in the air, you clap your hands. I could do finger push-ups.

My weight started coming down from 202 to 165. People said to me, "I bet you were dieting religiously while all of that was going on," and that is partially true, because I did quit eating in church.

As you're reading this, you could well be thinking, "This dude's trying to get me to lose weight." No, that is not the purpose of what I'm saying here. The purpose of this is to demonstrate the exact process of setting those goals.

Weight-Loss Tips

Incidentally, if you are really interested in losing weight, there are three things you need to do. Step number one, which is by far the most important: stay away from cottage cheese. A lot of people don't realize it, but cottage cheese is the most fattening food on earth. I have no scientific data to verify that, but I conclude that it has to be, because I've traveled almost all over the world, and I have noticed one constant thing: nobody but fat folks eat that stuff. So stay away from cottage cheese.

Number two, get a thorough physical examination, and number three, make certain it's from a skinny doctor. A fat doctor cannot tell you how to lose weight. Obviously they don't believe it's important, or they would have done something themselves.

Number four, get a positive doctor. What's a positive doctor? Most doctors, when they start talking to you about weight, will say, "Don't eat this, don't eat that, leave that alone. Don't touch that." I mean, if you like it, you can't have it. If you don't like it, eat all you want.

I love Dr. Martin's approach to eating proper food. He said, "Mr. Ziglar, you're going to be delighted to know that you can eat anything you want. As a matter of fact, I have made you a list of what you are going to want." He made it very simple for me.

There are a lot of different diets and a lot of different diet books. I happen to believe that *The Aerobics*

Program for Total Well-Being, by Dr. Kenneth H. Cooper, is a marvelous book on that subject.

I give you these details about losing weight simply because it gives you a example that we can follow all the way through in setting goals, and a goal properly set is at least partially reached.

The Step-by-Step Process

What is the step-by-step process? Let me give you the bad news first: it takes time to do this. As a matter of fact, in order to do this properly, to have a complete, well-balanced goals program, it's going to take you somewhere between ten and twenty hours. That's a lot of time. That discourages a whole lot of people, but I can absolutely guarantee you that what I'm suggesting you do is exactly what I do every day.

If you follow this procedure, you will save anywhere from two to as many as ten hours every week, which will enable you to do the things you really want to do. You will start realizing that time is your greatest asset, and the use of that time plays a major role in what you're able to get done in life. The bad news: it takes time to set these goals; the good news is that it saves you a lot of time.

Here's some more good news. If you can figure out what twelve times twelve is, you can also figure out what 2,865 times 9,412 is. That's because there is a precise formula that you follow. When you learn how to set a physical goal, you will now also know how

Following a step-by-step goals program you will save anywhere from two to as many as ten hours every week, which will enable you to do the things you really want to do.

to set a mental, spiritual, social, financial, or a family goal, because the procedure is exactly the same. There's no mystery to it. It is simply a procedure.

The Wild Idea Sheet

Step number one: in order to set your goals, you need to take a sheet of paper. I call it the Wild Idea Sheet. Print everything you want to be or do or have.

A lot of people say, "Well, now, Ziglar, that will take me three days." I can assure you that fully 90 percent of everything you want to be or do or have that's in your mind at this point will be on paper within an hour. Print down everything.

Why do I say to print these things? Printing requires more concentration, which burns it more deeply into the subconscious mind.

Now let me tell you what is by far the greatest benefit from following a goals program: you program your left brain, and that releases your creative right brain. If you follow these steps, you will be catapulted many steps forward.

The September-October 1992 issues of *Psychology Today* had a fascinating article about why Chinese math students do so much better than

American students. The prime reason given was that Chinese students learn their multiplication table until it becomes almost nauseating. Over and over, they drill them, drill them, and drill them. That left brain is completely programmed. If you wake one of them up at 2:30 in the morning and ask, "What is 23 times 31?" bang, they can give you the answer.

That simply programs the brain so carefully that when the students get into the abstract level, which requires creativity, they're infinitely more effective.

Let me give you a couple of examples. Michael Jordan, I believe, is one of the greatest athletes to ever live; he has tremendous athletic skills and so much creativity. Let me tell you why. He has spent thousands of hours learning all of the fundamentals: the dribble, the pass, the over-the-shoulder, the anticipation. When he gets in a situation he's never been confronted with before—and there's never been a game where every player is not confronted with something he's never been confronted with before—his technique is so fundamentally sound in his left brain that he is free to be creatively right-brained. Fortunately, he also has the athletic skill to follow through on that creativity.

One mistake that industry is learning now is that you can get promoted too fast. You can move up too quickly, before you have all the details so fundamentally sound in your left brain, so that your creativity is never really freed to come up with innovative new ideas.

Today it's the rage for top management to go to the bottom rung to ask questions about ways to improve. That's because those individuals have been doing their routine jobs thousands of times. They've come up with some creative ideas in the process, but because of their personality and position, and because of the closed-door policy of a lot of businesses, they do not want to go to the upper levels and say, "I've got an idea."

To return to our exercise: when you're printing what you want, you're really disciplining your left brain; you're learning thoroughly. That frees the right brain.

The second thing in setting those goals is to wait from twenty-four to forty-eight hours; personally I'm convinced that forty-eight hours is better. In that period, keep the list with you, because you will add a half dozen or a dozen other things to it.

At the end of the forty-eight hours, with each thing you've printed, ask yourself, "Why do I want to be or do or have this?" If you can't answer this question in one sentence, then at this time this really is not a viable goal for you to work on.

When I told the cafeteria story, I made the point that you can't eat everything on the cafeteria line. In life you can't have everything that is out there. In America, there are over fifty thousand ways to earn a living. You'd starve to death if you tried to do fifty thousand things to earn a living. You have to get focused.

"Say 'no' to the good, so we can say 'yes' to the best.
That's part of maturity. That's part of responsibility."
—Zig Ziglar

Our main objective now is to shorten that list. You can't be, do, and have everything. For example, you can't both be rude and nasty and have friends, both be a spendthrift and accumulate wealth, both eat French chocolate almond ice cream three times a day and be physically fit. You can't work all day and party all night. You can't golf or fish five days a week, spend three hours watching TV daily, and get your master's degree. You can't write a daily column and play on the company softball team. You can't attend all plays, games, and church socials.

Let me tell you about a little game I play. About every three years I do this, and its purpose is to say no to the good so we can say yes to the best. That's part of maturity. That's part of responsibility. That's part of making the right decisions and choices.

The last time I did this, I listed all the things I would like to do that year. Here's some of them: I wanted to conduct more family seminars. I wanted to start a daily radio program. I wanted to write a daily newspaper column. I wanted to campaign to get a lot of the advertising of booze, violence, and sex off television. I wanted to work in political campaigns to get qualified people in public office. I wanted to spend more time with my staff, write at least one book a year, learn how to speak Spanish, become more socially involved with neighbors, read and research a minimum of three and preferably four hours each day, spend an hour getting in physical condition, and be more active in civic and social clubs. I also wanted to set a record for people my age on the treadmill over at the Cooper Clinic. I wanted to go to Russia and China, and I wanted to play golf five days a week. When I put all of those things together and guesstimated the amount of time they would take, it came up to 368 hours a week. But there are only 168 hours in the week.

What do I have to do? I have to start eliminating the things that are not really important in my life, but until I put them all down, I might have been guilty of saying, "I want to do this, and I want to do this and that and the other." That's why so many people go through life frustrated.

Some Goals Must Be Big

One thing that concerns me about advertising is the promises they give you: if you will use this deodorant, or use this shaving cream or perfume, you will be irresistible to members of the opposite sex; if you will do this, you will go right to the top. That is an illusion, but if you repeat it often enough, it becomes believable. Unrealistic expectations are the seedbed of depression. Here we're trying to create a program that will enable us to know what we really want to do

---

Unrealistic expectations are the seedbed of depression.

---

in life and plan so that we have a legitimate chance of making it.

Psychology Today says that a twenty-year-old American today has ten times as much of a chance of being depressed as does his forty-year-old father, and twenty times the chance of being depressed as his sixty-year-old grandfather. Why? Unrealistic expectations.

At the same time, we need to realize that some goals must be big. Big goals create excitement.

I love the story of old "Gentleman" Jim Corbett. The heavyweight champion of the world was out doing his roadwork one morning. He saw a fisherman having a field day. He had pulled in little ones, he had pulled in big ones. With every cast, he'd pull in a fish, but Corbett noticed that he was throwing back the big fish and keeping the little ones. He had never seen that done before.

He ran over to the fisherman and said, "I love to fish myself. You're doing something I've never seen done before. You're throwing the big ones back and keeping the little ones. Why on earth are you doing it?"

The fisherman sadly shook his head, and said, "You don't know how I hate to do this, but I just don't have a choice. You see, all I have is this little bitty frying pan."

Before we laugh too loudly, let me emphasize a point: this story is talking about you and about me.

Many times we get the big dream, the big goal, the big idea. No sooner do we get it than we say, "Oh, no, Lord, don't give me such a big one. All I have is just this little bitty frying pan. Give me a small one. Besides, you know that's not a good idea. If it was, somebody else would have thought of it a long time ago."

Isn't it tragic that we have no more confidence in ourselves than this? Again, that's the purpose of this book—to build confidence. Then, when those big ideas hit you, you'll start working on them in such a way that you can get them done.

You also have to have some long-range goals. On Monday afternoon, I get onboard an aircraft headed for Miami. When I do, it's going to be going straight to Miami. Twenty minutes later, it will not be going to Miami, because the direction and the velocity of the wind will change. The gravitational pull of the earth, the moon, the sun, and the stars will pull it slightly off course, so the captain of the aircraft will turn it around, come back to Dallas–Fort Worth and land, and then we'll start over.

Do you believe what I've just said? What is the captain of the aircraft going to do? He's not going to change his decision to go; he's going to change his direction in order to get there.

You'd be amazed at the number of people who set an objective, encounter an obstacle, and then throw up their hands and say, "I guess I'm not supposed to do it." Instead of being creative and changing directions to get there, they abandon the goal itself.

Long-range goals help you to overcome short-range frustrations. I'm not going to be negative. I'd be like that little boy who came home from school one day and said, "Dad, I'm afraid I flunked my arithmetic test."

His dad said, "Son, that's negative. Be positive."

"Dad, I'm positive I flunked that arithmetic test."

I'm positive when I say this: You will have trouble, disappointments, defeats, reversals, and setbacks in your life. You think your kid's going to be the starting quarterback; he's not going to make the cut. You think you're going to make the big sale; you'll lose the last one you made. You think you're going to get the promotion; you'll be fired. You think everything is lovely only to discover that everything ain't lovely. That is part of life.

If you have a balanced long-range goals program, when something of that sort happens, you will regard it as a pebble on the beach—depending, of course, on the severity, but many times it simply is the pebble on the beach. But if you don't have real direction in your life, you think it's the whole oceanfront.

The rule is simply this: you go as far as you can see, and when you get there, you'll be able to see further.

Other Types of Goals

Some goals must be small, and they must be daily. That's the boring part, but it is also the most exciting part. It requires discipline, but every time you take a step forward, you realize that you are making progress. As the old saying goes, you can eat an elephant one bit at a time. The old saying is true: by the mile, it's a trial; by the inch, it's a cinch.

Some goals must be ongoing. For example, educational goals. An amazing number of people think that when they get their diploma or degree, their educational days are over. But that's when your education really begins. Building a healthy self-image is an ongoing goal, because you can have a marvelous self-image today, but disaster strikes tomorrow, and then you say, "I am a nothing. I am a nobody."

Building a better relationship with my mate, with my children is an ongoing goal. Getting better at my job is an ongoing goal.

Some goals could require consultation. Both our family and our company have a financial consultant. "Well, Ziglar, don't you know how to manage money?" No. Not as well as he does. So I need somebody to help in that direction.

When I went to see Dr. Martin, I knew I needed to lose weight. That was obvious. I had a picture of myself lying out on the diving board of my swimming pool—at least part of me was on the diving board. I knew that I needed to lose some weight; I just didn't know how much. He said, "Here is how much weight you need to lose." I was able to focus because it was specific, and it would involve small daily objectives.

I always go to another consultant when I have some things that I want to get done, particularly if they're very important. I do a lot of praying over them. I ask God, "Is this the goal for me?"

You may ask, "What does God say?"

He doesn't always say, "Yes, Zig, go do that," but I can tell you this: if it is not the right goal for me, he will not give me any peace about working toward it.

Most goals should be specific. They need to be specific, because when your goals are specific, things happen.

A number of years ago, I was onboard an aircraft flying over Niagara Falls. We were at about 30,000 feet, and the captain of the aircraft said, "Those of you who are seated on the right hand side of the aircraft, I'm going to tilt the plane slightly left. You should go and look at Niagara Falls."

The plane was about half empty, so I went to the left. Now thirty thousand feet is roughly six miles up in the air. That's a long way off, but even from six miles' distance, you could see the enormous power of 180 million gallons of water a minute flowing over those falls. The spray was coming up, and you could see it even at thirty thousand feet. You were impressed with the awesome power of Niagara Falls. Yet for years and years, that awesome power fell to the rocks below and dissipated into the distance.

Then one day a man came along and said, "I wonder what would happen if we did some construction here and took a small portion of that power, focused it on a specific point, got it to turn some wheels, and generated some hydroelectricity."

Bottom line: they have farmed millions of acres of ground. They've created thousands of jobs. They've educated children. They've built homes and schools and hospitals. They prospered simply because of that powerful focus. When we focus our lives, we unleash an incredible amount of power in our lives.

Check for Balance

Every one of these steps is designed to help you mark off some of the things you've previously written down. As I've said, you can't successfully have a hundred goals and work on them all at the same time. Check all of them for balance: physical, mental, spiritual, personal, family, career, social, and financial.

You might go down the list and ask yourself: If I reach every one of these goals, will I be happy, healthy, reasonably prosperous, and secure? Will I have friends, peace of mind, good family relationships, and hope in the future, or do I have it skewed toward one or two areas? Is there too much emphasis on the physical or the financial, with not enough for social or family goals? Ask yourself the question: do I have a balanced goals program?

You also need to ask yourself five basic questions. The first question: is this really my goal? Do I really want to drive a new Lincoln or a Lexus? Is that what

I really want, or do I want to get one because that sucker down the street has one?

Do I want to go to this university because it's the best university for me to get exactly what I want to further my career, or do I want to go there because a good friend of mine is going, and we want to go to the same school?

We have a lot of preachers, plumbers, lawyers, doctors, CPAs, and others who are not nearly as good as they could be because they're not doing what they really wanted to do. Their parents, their grandparents, their preachers, their professors had said, "You ought to be this." They really hadn't given it any further thought, and somebody else had set their goal.

The second question: is this really my goal? Is it morally right and fair to everyone concerned? You cannot be permanently happy at somebody else's expense. Nor can you be permanently happy if your goals violate the moral, ethical principles upon which society itself must rest.

The third question: will reaching this goal take me closer to or further from my major objective in life? As an example, if you're having financial difficulties, take questions number two and three and put them on a three-by-five card, put them in your pocket, so that every time you attempt to take your credit cards out, that's the first thing you'll see. Ask those questions: Is it morally right? Will reaching this goal, getting this, take me closer to or further from my major objective in life?

Let me tell you a story. A young man whom I'm very close to and love very much came to me when CDs and CD players first came out. He said, "Zig, can you get me discount on a CD player?"

"Probably."

"I'd sure like to get one of those things." This young man loves electronic gadgets, and if it has anything to do with music and if it's available, it has to be his.

I said, "Let me ask you a question before we buy it. Is it morally right and fair to everyone concerned?"

He thought about that for a moment and said, "Yes, I think it's morally right and fair to everyone concerned."

"OK, next question: will getting this CD player take me closer to or further from my major objective in life?"

He looked at me and said, "You just don't want me to have it."

"No," I said. "It's your deal."

The young man was a carpenter. His objective was to move up in the construction business. He wanted to be a subcontractor. In order to be a subcontractor, you have to have a lot of tools. He didn't have those tools. He didn't need to spend that money on a CD player. He needed to be buying tools.

I'm not going to tell you those two questions are the reason why all the following things happened, but I am going to be bold enough to say they played a part. Number one, he did not get the CD player.

---

5 Questions to Make Sure Your Goals are Balanced

1. Is this really my goal? Is this what I really want?
2. Is it morally right and fair to everyone concerned?
3. Will reaching this goal take me closer to or further away from my major objective in life?
4. Can I emotionally commit myself to starting and finishing this goal?
5. Can I see myself reaching this goal? Do I have a visual picture of myself reaching it?

Number two, today he's a superintendent with one of the three largest home builders in America, and in his state last year, the homes that he was in charge of represented 62 percent of all the homes they built.

When you begin to focus on what is important, when you ask those tough questions and answer them, that's when things happen in your life. Can I emotionally commit myself to starting and finishing this project? That is an enormously important one. Answer it honestly and sincerely.

Can I see myself reaching this goal? Do I have a visual picture of myself getting there? Very important. When you answer that question, things begin to happen.

Check for Negativity
Then we need to check for negativity. Goals need to be big, they need to be out of reach, but they don't

need to be out of sight, because if they are, you quickly realize you can't get there, you get discouraged, and you abandon the whole idea.

I'll give you a couple of examples. I was conducting a seminar in Detroit one time a number of years ago. The investment that was required for people to get into that franchise operation—it was a sales franchise—only required $2,500.

A young man came up to me after my goals seminar and said, "Man, I'm so excited. You have made me a million dollars. That's my goal for this year."

"Well, I hope you will share it with me, then."

He got a little irritated because he felt I was making fun of his goal. He said, "You don't believe I'm going to do it, do you?"

Here I'm faced with a very important ethical question. Do I exercise positive thinking and say, "You can do it," or do I look at the facts and counsel him on changing that objective?

Here are the facts: He's twenty-five years old. He's been working seven years. In that time, he's been unable to save $2,500. That's less than $400 a year. Now this year, he's going to make a million dollars? That's totally unrealistic. First he has to raise the $2,500 to buy the franchise.

"I'll tell you what let's do," I said. "Let's see if we can't break this down and determine whether or not that is a realistic goal." That's the process we're going through right now.

I had another young man whom I will never forget. He came to me and said, "My goal is to be the light heavyweight boxing champion of the world." He was thirty-one years old, and he weighed about thirty pounds too much for his height.

I asked him, "How much experience have you had?"

"I've never been in the ring, but my brother-in-law and I were out sparring the other day, and you can't believe how easily I handled him."

That young man would have gotten killed by even a fair amateur. We had to talk about different goals, like losing weight and getting in superb physical condition, and then look at an additional goal.

If goals are too big, they're negative. They're also negative if they're out of your field of study and basic interest.

I love good dentistry. One reason I do is simply that dentistry has had an important impact on my life. My teeth in my mouth get dirty, and I want to go to a dentist; I really do. But if I were to set being a dentist as my goal, that would be ridiculous. I'm not interested in that. My career would be getting started at least ten years from now. By then I'd be seventy-six years old. I'd only have thirty-five years left to practice. It simply would not be a logical thing. I have no interest in becoming a dentist.

Your goal can also be negative if you believe that luck is going to be the determining factor in reaching it.

Whom Do You Share Your Goals With?

A lot of times I've been asked, "Whom do you share your goals with?" Here is a basic answer: If it is a give-up goal, tell everybody. What's a give-up goal? "I'm going to quit drinking. I'm going to quit smoking. I'm going to quit cussing. I'm going to quit lying. I'm going to quit eating too much." If it's a give-up goal, you will find an enormous amount of support and encouragement. Everybody will say, "That's great. You can do it."

That's what the Twelve-Step programs are all based on. You go to those programs, and you hear other people say, "I did it. You can. Here's how." All of it is tied together. You share give-up goals with everybody. That strengthens your commitment and resolve, and the chances of reaching it go up.

On the other hand, you share your go-up goals very carefully. What's a go-up goal? "I'm going to be the starting quarterback. I'm going to write a best-selling novel. I'm going to write the greatest self-help book ever."

Let's say we have two salespeople, and one of them says to the other, "I'm going to be the number one salesperson in the company this year."

The other one says to herself, "In a pig's eye you are. *I'm* going to be the number one salesperson in the company."

Whom should you tell about that goal? Both of them should go to the sales manager and say, "Help

---

If it's a 'give up goal', share that goal with everybody;
if it's a 'go up goal', share it very carefully.

---

me devise a plan so I can be the number one salesperson." The sales manager will encourage you. Ideally, your mate will encourage you.

Share your goals with people whom you know are going to give you the encouragement that you need in order to get there.

Then you work the remaining goals through the process.

What do I mean when I say that? Whether the goal is to raise positive kids, get a better education, buy a new car, become the number-one salesperson, lose thirty-seven pounds, get a raise, acquire a new home, being a better mate or parent, or building a healthy self-image, you need to work them through the process.

The Steps of Goal Setting

1. Identify the goal.
2. List the benefits.
3. List the obstacles to overcome.
4. List the skills and knowledge required.
5. List the people or groups to work with.
6. Create an action plan.
7. Set the deadline for achievement.
8. Break the goal in pieces.
9. Have daily disciplined accountability.

Step number one, you identify that goal, and you write it down. For example, my original goal that we talked about earlier was to weigh 165 pounds and have a thirty-four-inch waistline. That's what I committed to in writing.

Step number two: I listed the benefits or reaching that goal. More energy. Less illness. For the first sixteen years after I got on this program, I missed one day of work because of illness. (That does not include the time my gallbladder ruptured, but that had nothing to do with what I was doing.) I would look and feel better. The redhead said I looked better after I lost that weight. Longer lifespan. All the statistics show that. Better endurance, and that certainly proved to be true. More productivity. Better attitude and disposition. More creativity. A better example to others.

I listed the benefits: why I want to lose that weight. It doesn't make any difference what the goal is: to get a better job, buy a new house, get a better education, or raise positive kids. You go through the process.

Step number three: what are the major obstacles to reaching this goal? It's amazing how we come up with a lot of excuses. "Bad weather; I can't do that."

I have jogged when it was forty degrees below zero. I've jogged when it was 115 out there. I've jogged when it was sleeting and snowing and during a rainstorm.

That's what was happening outside. Surely you don't think I was out in that kind of weather. Where was I? I was either jogging in place in my room, run-

ning up and down the corridor, or running in a park-
ing garage. I would find a place to run.

I have jogged in Alaska. I've jogged in London,
right across the street from Buckingham Palace. I've
jogged in South Africa on safari. I've jogged in numbers of places, but my point is when you've made the
commitment and you realize what the benefits are,
you're going to look at the problem and explore the
solution to it.

My schedule is irregular. Can I jog at the same
time every day? No way, but I've never had anybody
say to me, "Zig, when on earth can I find time to eat? I
mean, this is a problem with me. I am so busy, I never
have time to eat." You do what you schedule yourself
to do, and you schedule what is important.

I had terrible eating habits, especially late at
night—fried food, sweets. I was in poor physical condition. When you're in bad shape, you don't have any
energy to go out and get in shape, but I discovered an
astonishing thing.

When I started jogging, I could finish a seminar
absolutely exhausted, but I'd get out there and start
jogging. This would activate the pituitary gland and
flood the system with endorphins—nature's pain-
killer—and the dopamine and norepinephrine would
build up my endurance and energy.

What's the bottom line? I didn't have time *not* to
jog, because every thirty minutes I ran gave me an
additional two hours of high-voltage productivity.
It's not spending time; it's an investment.

Lack of discipline—that was the tough one for me.

When you discipline yourself to do the things you need to do when you need to do them, the days are going to come when you can do the things you want to do when you want to do them.

Skills and Knowledge

Step number four: what skill or knowledge is required to reach this goal? In this case, I only needed to know two things here about exercise and jogging. That's where the Cooper Clinic came in handy for me.

Step number five, who are the individuals, groups, companies, and organizations to work with? Dr. Ken Cooper, Dr. Randy Martin, and obviously the redhead and I have to agree on when is the best time. Sometimes I would come in at 6:00. She'd say, "Honey, I am so hungry. Can we eat now?"

I wanted to run, so I'd go ahead and do the dinner with the redhead, and then I'd run a couple of hours later on that evening. You have to keep everything in balance.

I have one friend who gets up every morning at 5:00 and runs an hour. He never has any time in the morning to spend with his family. You have to fit your goal in so you don't alienate the people who are important to you. That's the reason for the complete goals program.

When I schedule a speaking engagement, I frequently get invited to have a meal with the person

---

"When you discipline yourself to do the things you need to do when you need to do them, the days are going to come when you can do the things you want to do when you want to do them." —Zig Ziglar

---

sponsoring that engagement. My secretary always says, "Let's see how we work it around so he has time to do his exercising." That is a part of the schedule.

What is my plan of action to reach the goal? The most important thing is I had to make the commitment.

I also had to limit my sweets. I am not about to completely eliminate sweets. While I was in the process of losing this weight, I would have my dessert one day a week after church. I couldn't wait to get over to Braum's to get French chocolate almond ice cream. It happens to be the best ice cream in the world.

As you know if you've ever been in an ice cream parlor, there are some scoopers who are better than others. Some really get it up, and some are hesitant about giving you a full scoop.

So I would watch, and I would spot the best scooper, and if another scooper approached me to dip my ice cream, I'd always have my back turned; then, when I could see that the good scooper was available, I'd turn around, and I'd say I'd have a double dip of that French chocolate almond ice cream.

Oh, I tell you, I love my sweets. It became a goal to get there on Sunday and eat dessert, and then I'd set the goal to be there again the next Sunday. Since then, a lot of good things have been happening. Some of the yogurt today is just as good as that ice cream, without all that fat.

No fried foods. I don't think I've had three bites of fried food in the last three years. Exercise daily. I eat nutritional snacks late at night. I eat a well-balanced diet. I eat slowly, I only eat at the table, and I drink eight glasses of water every day. Those things have worked for me. When I had gone through all of the process, then I could put the completion date on it.

Organize Your Goals

I can't tell you the number of times I've had some-body say, "You have to have goals. As a matter of fact, by next October, I'm going to have X." They set an objective, and then they start trying to work things out in order to reach it on that date. That's a blueprint for disaster, because you become obsessed with that goal and you begin to neglect a lot of other things.

When you put your goals together as a program, you might discover that it's unrealistic to have that new automobile by next October. June the following year might be better, because you can do that in con-junction with everything else.

Again, when you organize your goals, you don't give up the things that are important just to get the things you want.

Setting your goals eliminates many of the goals that had been there before. What do you do then?

You choose four goals that you can work on every single day. What do you do with all of the others? You might have fifteen or twenty left.

I have a number of goals that I cannot work on every day. For example, one of my long-range goals is to play the top hundred golf courses in America. Of course I can't do that every single day, but every few weeks I'll play on one of the top hundred golf courses. Have I abandoned that goal because I can't work on it every day? Of course not.

I always write three books at one time. Obviously I can't do that, so what am I talking about? I start the research five years earlier. Every time I see an article or piece of information on the subject, I file it away. I clip the magazines and newspapers. I might not clip one article a week or even a month, but the idea is in front of me periodically at least every month.

I review all my goals to make certain I have them there, but on a weekly basis, I choose four that I'm going to work on every day. In two minutes at the end of the week, I can review them, and I can say it was a good week for this one, although I didn't do very much on this one (and sometimes that's going to happen). I am constantly reminded of where I am. This permits me to do more of the things I really want to do.

Early on, this process is going to require considerable discipline, but if you do it for thirty days, I'll guarantee that you'll be amazed, elated, motivated, enthusiastic, and grateful, because you will see changes take place in every aspect of your life.

You may be asking, "Ziglar, you say it takes time to set goals. How much time does it take on a daily basis to follow though?" Very important question. Here's what it takes me. At the beginning of the first of the week, either Sunday night or early Monday morning, I take thirty minutes to figure out the four most important goals I want to work on this week.

After that, each day it takes me roughly ten minutes. I simply keep a schedule of how long I spent doing one thing and how long I spent doing the other. At the end of the day, I sum it up. Then I can evaluate immediately whether I have accomplished my objectives for that day. I give myself a grade on each one, either a plus or a minus.

Do I expect a plus on every one of them every day? Obviously not. For example, I do not want a plus on my social goals every day. That would mean I was spending too much time visiting instead of getting things done.

At the end of the week, with the ones I do not reach, I mark the minus in red. That way I can instantly look. If I have too much red, I'll look where I got it, and I'll know whether or not I really had an effective week.

Progress Requires Change

How do you reach all of those goals? You start by recognizing that they're going to involve change. Not all change is progress, but there's not going to be progress without some change.

Can a person change? Yes, they emphatically can change. I'll tell you a story. I have a close friend named Ike Reighard. For the first four years of his life, he was in Appalachia. When he was four years old, his dad, who worked in quarries and pulp mills, moved the family to inner-city Atlanta.

Ike became the first member of his family to ever graduate from high school. He decided he was going to go to college. His family thought that was ridiculous. His friends pooh-poohed the idea. Here's a kid from Appalachia raised primarily in inner-city Atlanta: "Ike, you're kidding yourself." "No, I'm going to go to college."

Ike went to college, and the first year he flunked out royally. Like a lot of people, Ike said, "No big deal," and he did not go back the next year. He became a disc jockey at a very low-power station. He loaded and unloaded trucks. He did a lot of menial jobs. He was out of school for six years, struggling for survival.

Not all change is progress, but there's not going to be progress without some change.

Then Ike picked up a copy of my book *See You at the Top*. For the first time in his life, he learned something about self-image and about goals. For the first time, he believed that yes, he could do something with his life. He decided he was going to go back to college.

Ike applied at Mercer University in Macon, Georgia. They respectfully declined that request. He applied again, and this time he went in person to plead his case. They still said, "Ike, there's no way. You've been out of high school now six years. You flunked miserably the first go-around. There is no way."

As Ike was walking out of the room, terribly despondent, he bumped into Jean Hendricks, who was in charge of admissions. She could see that he was troubled and asked him what the problem was. He wept in front of her. He said, "I want so badly to get my education. I am now ready to get that education. They're not letting me back in."

Because of his openness (and frankly I'm certain those tears played a major part), she said, "OK, Ike. I'm going to let you in school very conditionally. If you do not maintain a B average at the end of this year, your education at Mercer is all over."

Two years and three months later, Ike Reighard graduated magna cum laude. Today, within a thirty-minute drive of inner-city Atlanta, where Ike Reighard was raised, he pastors one of the fastest-growing churches in this country. Ike Reighard does a lot of youth seminars. He is making a dramatic difference in a lot of lives. He says again and again that you can change.

One definition of insanity is to think you can keep on doing what you've been doing and somehow get different results. That simply is not going to work. You have to have the willingness to change. You have to have a vision. When Alexander the Great had a vision, he conquered the world. When he lost the vision, he couldn't conquer the liquor bottle. When David had a vision, he conquered Goliath and the Philistines. When he lost the vision, he could not even conquer his own lust.

With your direction set, it's astonishing how much more you can do.

Next, make the commitment. When you make a commitment and you encounter a problem, you immediately start looking for a solution to the problem. Without the commitment, you start looking for an escape from that problem.

Sam Walton, the founder of Walmart, said, "Commit to your business." I think I overcame every single one of my personal shortcomings by the sheer passion I brought to my work.

A Foundation of Integrity

If you're going to reach all of your goals, you have to build a solid foundation. That foundation must of necessity be built on integrity and honesty. It has to be built on the right qualities; otherwise you might reach some of your goals, but you won't reach them all.

A number of years ago, I had the privilege of going atop Calgary Tower in Calgary, Canada. That structure is 626 feet above the ground. I knew that was two football fields plus twenty-six more feet. That is way up there.

According to the recording you hear in the elevator when you go to the top, the structure weighs thirteen thousand tons, and seven thousand of those tons are underground. When you have a foundation like that, you can go high.

Alan Bean, one of the astronauts who walked on the moon, is a friend of mine. He's one of the men who stayed on that space platform fifty-seven days as it encircled the earth. He invited us to fly over to watch the blastoff. It is a spectacular sight.

I was talking with Alan about it, and he said, "Zig, if you think all of the gear and apparatus was spectacular, you should see what you couldn't see. The tons and tons of concrete from which the blastoff took place are absolutely wonderful. With a foundation like that, you can go anywhere in the world you want."

The foundation has to be solid. A good architect can come to downtown Dallas, downtown LA, or anywhere else, look at a hole in the ground, and tell you how big, how wide, and how tall the building is going to be. The foundation is the determining factor.

Today many people confuse success with popularity or fame. Madonna has one; Mother Teresa has the other. People often equate success with money or recognition, but I know many people with a lot of money who are not very happy. I also know many people who get a lot of publicity who are not very happy.

You might think about the richest man in town. You might say, "He really is a successful individual," but when you check up on all of what he has, how happy he is, what kind of family relationship he has, how many friends he has, how much peace of mind he has, it might look very different. I'm talking about winning the whole ball game, and the foundation is the important thing.

Focus on Attitude

Next, you need to make certain your attitude is good. Let me tell you one thing I do: I read the daily paper. I concentrate on the positive things. I turn to the comics section. I also read the sports. In virtually every athletic event, 50 percent of the participants are winners. When you think about it, that's a pretty high winning percentage.

Dennis the Menace is one of my favorite comics. In one, Dennis is in the car with his parents, and he's saying, "I didn't go to the bathroom before we left because I wanted to have something to do later." Most every parent in America can relate to that one.

If you really want to get a laugh, these only come out on Friday. You need to cut them out and save them for over a period of time. It's the weekly summaries of the soaps. I do not personally believe that you can watch the soaps every day and be both optimistic and morally sound—not both of them. But I can guarantee you if you enjoy a good laugh, and if you want to feel good about how your life is going, get the weekly summary of the soap operas.

Here's one summary of a week of *All My Children*:

Nick learns from Mona that Erica became pregnant after being raped as a teenager by a friend of her father's and that Mona put up the baby for adoption. Erica never saw the baby, and the matter was never discussed again. Kendall's birthmark makes Mona believe that Kendall is that baby. When Nick breaks into Kendall's room to get evidence, Kendall catches him. When Erica tells Nick to keep out of her employee's business, Nick hires Charlie to investigate. Meanwhile, as Erica brags about her perfect child, Bianca, Kendall fumes.

Gloria turns down Adam's proposal to marry right away. Mimi tells Tom the secret about her baby just before they walk into a surprise party. Losing control, Mimi throws everybody out, which makes Taylor suspicious. Tad is back in town but fails to see eye-to-eye with Dixie. Dixie sees Brooke and Tad kiss.

If you really want to have a good attitude, cut these summaries out, save them, and read one every day the next week. It will do wonderful things for you.

What are some other ways of building a good attitude? When you're growing, when you're doing things, when you have your goals set and are working on them, when you're building your self-improvement—those are some of the greatest things for your attitude.

Some people labor under the illusion that you have to like everything about your job and that you have to enjoy doing everything about your job. Nothing could be further from the truth.

I love my work; I don't believe there's a human being alive who enjoys doing what they do as much as I do. But do I like everything about it? No, I don't, but if I have to do something, I have a choice to make. Am I going to do it with the right attitude and get better results, or am I going to gripe and moan and fuss about it and get worse results? That is the choice I have to make.

Of course, the decision was already made when you took the job. But you're going to discover this: the better your attitude is toward the things you don't really like to do, the more likely you are to be given more of the things you do like to do. Even so, every-

---

When you have to do something, you have a choice to make. Am I going to do it with the right attitude and get better results, or am I going to gripe and moan and fuss about it and get worse results? That is the choice you have to make.

---

thing is not going to be dessert. There are still going to be unpleasant aspects to your job.

I think of Tom Hartman. I think of all of those months that he spent losing weight. I know that there were many times when he did not feel like exercising while carrying all that weight, and yet, because he had made the commitment, he had the vision, and the picture was so clear, he stayed with it.

What's the final result? The last time I saw Tom Hartman, he weighed roughly 225 pounds. Now, here's a man six feet, four inches tall, with a large frame. He can easily carry that and not be overweight.

Tom graduated magna cum laude with a degree in psychology. He made his contribution counseling battered women. He had his own business and was doing infinitely better. He was teaching a Sunday School class every Sunday.

Initially Tom was not happy; the last time I saw him, he was. He had not been healthy; when I saw him, he was. He had not been prosperous; he is. He has great peace of mind, with a tremendous number of friends. He has marvelous family relationships. He has tremendous hope that the future is going to be even better.

I keep bringing his case up for this simple reason: I don't believe there's a person who will ever read this book who has as much to overcome in every area of life as Tom Hartman did. Yet by making that commitment and following through, he achieved absolutely spectacular results. Ensure your attitude.

Did Tom learn something every one of the five hundred times he listened to those tapes? Of course not, but let me tell you something that is at the same time enormously exciting and tremendously frightening. He memorized them. He said he would sit there, and he would go right along with me word for word. Let me tell you what he was doing: he was self-talking, and the most important things you will ever hear are what you say to yourself. He was being encouraged. That's the reason that repetition is so important. He made the commitment. He didn't wait to get down. He didn't gamble on it every day. He did what was necessary to stay up. He was ensuring his attitude.

Tom also made it a habit to do something for somebody else. The people I talk with who are the happiest are those who are doing things for other people as a matter of course. It is absolutely true, as I have emphasized, that you can have everything in life you want if you will just help enough other people get what they want.

Daily Disciplined Accountability

To reach your goals, you also have to have daily disciplined accountability. Consider the United States Marines: 175 former Marines are the CEOs of Fortune 500 companies; twenty-six of our presidents served in the military. In the military, they teach discipline and commitment. These two really do go together.

Let me make a point here. Exceptions will kill you. I have a close friend, the most positive man I've ever known in my life. His name is Bernie Lofchick. He had quit smoking for five years, and then one day said, "You know, it smells so good, and one won't hurt." It took him five years more to get off permanently, and the last time he quit was about fifteen years ago. I'm telling you: don't make the exception.

Some psychiatrists say that under certain conditions, some alcoholics could go back and have a social drink. That borders on insanity. Why gamble with something like that? I have seen many cases where a person was sober for a number of years; then they took that one drink, just a glass of wine or one beer that's not going to hurt anything, and they were back off to the races. Watch for those exceptions.

One day I spoke in Seattle. I left Dallas that morning. I flew all the way to Seattle, spoke, and flew back to Dallas. When I got home, by the time I'd collected all my stuff and got ready to hop in bed, it was 4:00 in the morning.

My clock was set to get up at 5:30. It didn't take me long to figure out that that was one hour and a half. I don't need to tell you that ninety minutes of sleep is not nearly enough. Although the clock was already set for 5:30, as I sat there on the side of the bed, I debated: do I pull the plug and get up at 5:30, or do I sleep in?

"Be smart, Ziglar. Sleep in." Every fiber of my being said don't get up at 5:30, but I'd made a commitment; I'd pulled the plug. I got up at 5:30. I did my jogging. I had an absolutely miserable jog and had an absolutely horrible day. I was not nearly as productive that day as I normally am. I didn't feel good all day long. I was in bed that night at 8:00. Yet one of the most important decisions I've ever made in my life was to get up at 5:30. Let me tell you why: had I bowed to my physical, emotional, and mental desire to sleep in, I would have made that exception. A week later, I might have made an exception if I was only going to get four hours of sleep. A week later, maybe I'd make the exception if I had only gotten seven hours of sleep, and the exception would be repeated so many times that it would become the rule. Had I slept in, I would have faced that danger.

Watch those exceptions. Do you never make exceptions? Yes, on occasion you do, but the instant you do, be completely aware of it, and write yourself a little note. Watch out, because that is a danger signal. That daily disciplined accountability of working your goals every day can make a difference.

You need to stay in shape physically, mentally, and spiritually, because man is physical, mental, and spiritual. Here is another rather intriguing phenomenon. Even though we have spent billions of dollars in the last ten years on health programs, exercise programs, diet books, and diet programs, our obesity rate is 6 percent higher than it was ten years ago.

This is why I say I believe more people have permanently lost weight reading my materials and listening to my recordings than they have with diet and exercise books: because we deal with the big picture. Visualize what you really do want; look at the benefits from taking care of your health.

According to one major study, 92 percent of the CEOs of major corporations had very high energy levels. According to another study, 90 percent of them exercise regularly. Less than 10 percent of them smoke, most of them can tell you their cholesterol level, integrity is their number-one asset, and their families are their number-one priority. In other words—balance. Stay in shape physically, mentally, and spiritually.

---

4 Fast Rules for Staying in Shape Physically

1. Get enough sleep. Despite what I said previously, this is very important.
2. Get on a regular diet and a sensible eating and exercise program.
3. Avoid the poisons: drugs, alcohol, and smoking. Keeping the poisons out of your system is a marvelous way to stay in better shape. You will feel better.
4. Visualize yourself being in better shape. That's when it will come to be.

Failure is the line of least persistence. There's going to come a time in all of our lives when we hit the wall. Marathon runners talk about it all the time: "I hit the wall. I ran completely out of energy, and that's when I ran on instinct."

A lot of times we do that. We do not have any reserve left, but if we make the commitment, we can go on. Please don't misunderstand: if you're having a heart attack, lie down and call the doctor. But many people quit at the first sign of discomfort. They simply do not hang in there, and hanging in there gets to be very important. When you're in good shape, you can call on that extra energy when you need it, and it takes discipline beforehand in order to get there.

Change Your Vocabulary

If you want to reach your goal, you also need to change your vocabulary. I never will forget the spring day I was in Portland, Oregon, jogging on Portland State University campus. The temperature was about 78 degrees. I had a seminar that afternoon, and as I was running that day, I suddenly realized something: I was feeling good. The ground was flowing smoothly beneath my feet. I was breathing easily.

I mention that because for nearly ten months, when that opportunity clock would sound off in the morning, I can't tell you the number of times I'd gotten up, put my running clothes on, and gone outside. And while I was running, I was fussing: "Ziglar, what are you trying to do? You're killing yourself acting like a teenager. Your buddies are sound asleep in bed or having a good time. What are you trying to prove?"

As I've said many times, you have to pay the price. I'll tell you, it was awful, but I'd made up my mind

---

You don't pay the price for good health,
you enjoy the benefits of good health.

---

that I was going to do it, and if I said I was going to do it, I would. I told every friend, relative, neighbor, and complete stranger about the terrible sacrifice I was making, but I said I was going to do it, and I was.

Now here I am in Portland, Oregon, and I'm out there running, and all of a sudden, I'm feeling good. The ground is flowing easily. I'm breathing smoothly. I'm having a wonderful time, and that's the day I changed my vocabulary.

You don't pay the price for good health; you enjoy the benefits of good health. You don't pay the price for success; you pay the price for failure. You enjoy the benefits of success. You don't pay the price for a good marriage; you enjoy the benefits of a good marriage. You pay the price for a bad one.

When we discipline ourselves to keep on, the day is going to come when instead of being a chore, our job gets to be fun. I believe that you can make almost any job fun to do.

In North Carolina, there is a chicken-plucking plant that uses these concepts. As a youngster, I was a butcher, and I'm here to tell you that when you pull the feathers off one chicken and when you're cleaning all those chickens out, the inside of one chicken looks just like the inside of all the others. When you've seen one, you've seen them all.

Now can you imagine? Here's a group of people who are cleaning chickens, at minimum wage in virtually every case, and the managers started developing those people. They started giving them ear sets and motivational recordings, and the workers started listening. They'd be listening along; when I'd put a funny on the tape, they would laugh and go back to cleaning chickens.

Productivity went up substantially. Turnover reduced substantially. Profits increased substantially.

What am I saying? Everybody gets excited when they're having some fun, when we're taking an interest in them, and when we're developing their interest.

We've gotten business because the owner of that plant went all over that part of North Carolina, speaking at Lion's Clubs and Rotaries and telling them what his hourly workers were doing.

Many times we think, "That person is not interested in this kind of stuff," or "You can't motivate that person." Let me tell you something: when people have fun doing what they're doing, they're going to do a better job. Again, that's not to say that everything can be fun.

Break the Goal in Pieces

Step number eight is to break the goal in pieces. After I left the Cooper Clinic, and they said to me, "Here's what you have to do," I looked at it and planned on losing the weight in ten months. I figured that would be how long it would take to write my book *See You at the Top.* I was doing them simultaneously. I needed to lose thirty-seven pounds, so I divided that up and said, "All I have to do is lose 3.7 pounds a month."

That's no big deal. That's less than a pound a week. I knew that, and I knew that I knew that I could do it. I was so confident of it that I didn't even bother to get started for twenty-eight days. That's one of the major problems in life. Here's your quota: it's for six months. "Hey, that's no big deal. It's just February 23. I have plenty of time." The next thing you know, it's March 22, and then it's April 15. "Oh, it's too late now, but next year, I guarantee you . . ."

I looked at my regimen again and discovered that in order to lose the thirty-seven pounds, all I had to do was lose 1.9 ounces a day on average, every day, for ten months.

See You at the Top has 384 pages. I wrote it in ten months. That means on average, I wrote one and a quarter pages a day, every day, for ten months.

Let me tell you how to raise positive kids in a negative world. Let me tell you how to build a magnificent relationship with your mate. Let me tell you how to move to the top of the corporate ladder. Let me tell you how to become a world-class professional salesperson, counselor, educator, or whatever you want to be. It is not the monumental task that you do for one week or one month. It's the daily things that you do, the daily commitment: "Today I'm going to take this step, or that step. I'm going to make this kind of progress every day." The little things make a difference.

A minute can make a difference. If you don't think a minute is important, let me tell you that depends on which side of the bathroom door you are. One minute can absolutely make a lot of difference. If my watch is four hours wrong, I have no problem. If I wake up at 3:00 in the morning and if it's four hours wrong, I can tell you instantly that it's wrong. If it's four minutes wrong, that's a different story.

Say I'm due to get aboard an aircraft at 2:32. If I'm four minutes wrong and I get there at 2:36, you know what the problem is. See, I've made a deal with the airlines: if I'm not there when they get ready to go, they're just to go ahead without me. Now I'm here to tell you, folks, that it's easier to catch those dudes before they leave the ground. The little things make the big difference.

Team Playing

If you're going to reach your goals, you have to be a team player. You have to join the team; you have to work with others.

When I was a youngster down in Yazoo City, Mississippi, there were some abandoned railroad tracks. On occasion we kids used to go over there and see which of us could walk the furthest on those tracks.

We'd walk a few steps and fall off. Had we just joined hands across the rails, we could have walked as far as the tracks went by supporting and balancing each other.

You have to have the team concept. Although many say that job security no longer exists, employment security is a thing of an entirely different nature. The better team player you are, the better individual you are, the better performer you are, the more likely you are to have employment security.

Have you ever seen a flock of Canadian geese flying overhead? If you follow them very far, you will notice that they always fly in a V formation. If you follow them all across the horizon, you will also notice that there periodically appears to be some confusion in the flock.

Why do the geese fly in the V formation? Wind tunnel tests have revealed that when they do, they set up a partial vacuum off either wing, so the flock can fly 73 percent further than the individual goose can.

The reason for that apparent confusion from time to time is that the lead goose, in fighting the headwind, grows weary more quickly, so they change the leader's position very frequently. They cooperate. They work together.

Incidentally, a few years ago some psychologists studied geese, and they discovered that when you hear them honking, they're not just honking "Dixie." Those are motivational honks; those are encouragement honks. They're saying, "Come on, Bill. You know Charlie Brown's farm is just four miles down the road. Man, you can make it. Hang in there. It's downwind all the way."

That's partly because of the loyalty the geese have for each other. If one of them gets hurt or sick, a companion will stay with them until they either recover or die. Loyalty—a moral principle.

Training Fleas

If you're going to reach your goals, you have to learn how to train fleas. (Incidentally, I know you've heard the one about the two fleas at the bottom of the hill; one of them said, "Do we walk, or shall we take a dog?")

You train fleas by putting them in a jar; you put the top on. The fleas will jump up, and they'll hit the top over and over. You watch them jump and jump, and then you will notice that although they continue to jump, they're no longer hitting the top. At that point you can take the top off. They will continue to jump, but they cannot jump out of the jar, because they have conditioned themselves to jump just so high.

Man is exactly the same way. He starts out in life to write the book, to break the record, to climb the mountain, to do something significant. Along the way, he bumps his head, stubs his toe, makes some mistakes, and all of a sudden, he loses that marvelous concentration and confidence and creativity. He becomes a *SNIOP*—a person who is *Susceptible to the Negative Influence of Other People.*

In case you're missing the point, flea trainers are people who jump out of a jar. They don't tell other people where to get off; they show them how to get on. Flea trainers understand that you don't try to see through people; you try to see people through. They understand that you can have everything in life you want if you will just help enough other people get what they want.

If you want to reach your goals, you have to have that flea trainer attitude. You have to understand that just because somebody else did or didn't accomplish something has nothing whatever to do with your abilities.

The classic example is the four-minute mile. For years and years, athletes had said, "I'm going to break the four-minute barrier." When they did, the coaches would get their stopwatches out and say, "Man, you might get it down to 4:02, but you'll never break that barrier." The doctors were saying, "Your heart will come right out of your body. There is no way you can ever run a mile in less than four minutes." For years and years, athletes tried valiantly to do it, but could not.

Then one day a flea trainer named Roger Bannister from Britain ran a mile in less than four minutes. Almost immediately after him, John Landy of Australia broke the four-minute barrier, and since then over five hundred individuals have run that race in

---

Avoid becoming a *SNIOP*: A person who is *Susceptible to the Negative Influence of Other People*.

---

less than four minutes, including a high-school student and a thirty-seven-year-old man. In 1985, John Walker of New Zealand, became the first man in history to run one hundred sub-four-minute miles.

There have been any number of races in which eight young men, all in the same race, broke the four-minute barrier. Is it because they all suddenly got that much better physically? Did the equipment improve that much? It might have improved some, but Roger Bannister followed every principle of goal setting that I'm talking about here.

Number one, he was a superb athlete. Number two, he got in marvelous condition. Number three, he recruited three other guys to serve as his pacers in that race, and he had targets along the way. He knew how long his strides were, how many he could jog or run in four minutes. He broke it all down. When he broke the barrier, athletes all over the world realized it was not a physiological barrier, it was a psychological one. That's an important difference.

I've seen it happen many times. A salesperson breaks a record, and then somebody comes along and says, "If she can, I can." That example serves as an inspiration. That's the reason I tell so many stories. In addition, the Center for Creative Leadership in

Greensboro, North Carolina, has discovered beyond any doubt that the parable, the story, is the best way to teach. Of course, that's something somebody else told us two thousand years ago, isn't it?

See the Reaching

Next: if you're going to reach your goals, you have to see the reaching. Jack Nicklaus says he gets his best golf practice on his way to the golf course. He has a detailed outline of the course itself, and he sees every shot before he ever hits it. He sees the ball going in the hole.

I saw myself doing exactly what I'm doing way back yonder in 1952. It took me sixteen more years before I could do it on a full-time basis, and in those years I had to do a lot of other things. I worked as a salesperson to support my family, but the dream, the vision, never left me. I could see myself there.

When I hung that fellow in the Jockey shorts on my bathroom mirror, I saw him hundreds and hundreds of times, and I kept saying, "Now that's the way I am going to be." I could see the reaching.

Years ago, when the sailing ships were on the seas, a young sailor was ordered aloft; a squall was coming up. As he was ordered aloft, he was to trim the sails. When he was climbing up, he made the mistake of looking down. The turbulence of the sea and the roll of the ship caused him to become nauseated. He started to lose his balance. An older sailor underneath him said, "Look up, son, look up." He looked up and regained his balance.

If the outlook is not looking good, try the uplook. It's always good. Helen Keller put it eloquently when she said, "If you keep your eyes on the sun, you will not see the shadows."

We need to see ourselves as already being there. We need to see ourselves as happy in our relationships with our mate and our children. If we see our students in the proper light, we will deal with them altogether differently. You treat people exactly as you see them, and the way you treat them has a direct bearing on their performance.

I can tell you that as a parent that parental expectation has a direct bearing on children's performance. I can tell you as an employer that employer expectation has a direct bearing on employees' performance. I can tell you as an educator that my expectation of those I'm teaching has a direct bearing on their performance.

If you're going to reach those goals, you need to do it now. *Tomorrow* has been described as the greatest labor-saving device of all time. We use it often: "I'm going to do this tomorrow. I'm going to do this when I have time. I'm going to do this when . . ."

"If you keep your eyes on the sun, you will not see the shadows." —Helen Keller

---

The present is now. The future is also now. We need to get into action. I've done such a strong job of selling you on having goals because I know that if you take action now, you're going to be infinitely more successful. You're far more likely to reach your goals. If you have those goals, if you can see them, that's when things are going to happen, but you have to get started now.

Andy at Merrill Lynch

One of my favorite examples is the story of Andy Gardner. He's a young man who works with Merrill Lynch, a company that is said to have more people who earn $100,000 a year than any other company in America.

Andy said to me, "Zig, they come in all sizes, all shapes, all colors. They're extroverts and introverts. They're male and female. They have tremendously varied educational backgrounds. Some of them offer the complete menu; others are specialists, but there's one thing that every one of them has in common: you call them at 2:30 in the afternoon on February 22 or March 23 and ask them where they are on their goals, and they can, to the penny, tell you exactly. They're very definite, they're very specific in their goals."

Andy said to me, "Zig, I started listening to you a number of years ago. Here's what I discovered. You and I come from a different generation. We have different political views. We have different social views. We have different religious views, but the principles that you're talking about are so universal that I adopted every one of them and am following them as a part of my life."

Let me tell you Andy's story. When you join Merrill Lynch, one of the first objectives they have is to make the Executive Club. That's kind of a rookie club, and making it early on represents a considerable amount of recognition for accomplishment.

Andy's manager was a man named Parks Duncan. Parks called him in one day. "At that point," said Andy, "I wasn't on schedule to make anybody's club. Parks got to talking to me, and he said, 'Andy, let me tell you what I'm going to do. I believe you have every ability to make the Executive Club, and I want to show you where your new office is going to be. We're building it about a half mile from here. Here's the blueprint and, Andy, here is your office.'"

Andy left Parks's office. He was so excited that he skipped lunch and walked a half mile over to the new building, which was nothing but a frame and a lot of concrete and girders. He knew exactly where his office was. He said, "Only the floor was in. I got there, and I squatted down as if I were at my desk. I looked out, and the view was absolutely marvelous. I visualized my sales assistant outside answering the phone saying, 'Yes, this is Mr. Gardner's office.' I could see all of that in my own mind."

Now this is the kind of visualization that I've been talking about. Andy said, "You know, Zig, when I left there, I had that dream. I had a vision. Yes, I was going to make the Executive Club. In the month of November, I more than doubled my daily production." He said, "I just was so excited I was on schedule to make it."

Then, he said, "Early in December, all three of my big deals washed out. At that point some of my associates were saying to me, 'Andy, you really ought to start concentrating on next year.'

"But," he said, "by then it was absolutely impossible for me to give up. I took that renewed effort. I started going over to the new office I was going to be in every day. The vision became more real all the time, and it's amazing how things started popping in place. The goal was to get there on December 21, and on December 21 is exactly when I hit my goal."

Visualization does work. This happened to Andy back in 1984. Three years later he moved to Houston, and for two and a half years he managed an office there. Then, he said, "I felt like I needed an explosion."

Andy came to Dallas and spent three days with us in June 1992. Even though he'd lost three days of productivity, a larger picture of himself and his vision emerged, and as a result of that, not only did he make the President's Club, which is infinitely more prestigious, in that month of June, he broke his best record ever by over 80 percent. In July, he almost broke the

June record, and August was a repeat of the same thing.

Since then, he set another goal, and when that happened, he decided he would win the company's Winsmith Award. He accomplished that objective too.

Let me emphasize something that is very important: Had Andy made the Winsmith Award his first goal, that would have been absolutely insane. He had no experience, and he had a very small base to work from. He was just getting started. There were many things he did not know. He set a more reasonable goal—a big goal, but it wasn't out of sight. He achieved it: he made the Executive Club.

Andy's three best years were 1990, 1991, and 1992. Yet those were far from the best economic years in our society. That goes right back to something I've been saying all the way through: Success is not out there. Success is right between your ears.

I don't care how good times are; some people are going to foul them up financially. I don't care how bad times are; some people are going to do well regardless. I've noticed that since the Depression way back in the 1930s.

I believe that if you'll take the steps we've been discussing and follow this goal setting procedure, success can be yours.

As you start on this journey, there are going to be some people who will laugh at you and say, "Man, you can't do it," just as they did to Andy Gardner and Ike Reighard.

The little world laughed, but the big world was on the banks of the Hudson when Robert Fulton went steaming by. The little world laughed, but the big world was at Kitty Hawk when the Wright Brothers made that historic flight into space. The little world laughed, but the big world was tuned in when Alexander Graham Bell made that historic phone call.

The little world might well laugh at you as you start out on your journey, but the big world is going to be right by your side, encouraging you as you go, and it will be there to greet you as you cross the finish line.

And remember: what you get by reaching your goals is not nearly as important as what you will become by reaching your goals. That is the winner you were born to be.

"The little world might well laugh as you start out on your journey, but the big world is going to be right by your side, encouraging you as you go, and it will be there to greet you as you cross the finish line." —Zig Ziglar

---

Chapter 4

Winning through Persistence, Enthusiasm, and Desire

There was an old boy down home who was caught in a flash flood. I mean, it was an instant one, and he was up on the rooftop of his house. One of his neighbors came floating by and said, "John, this flood is just terrible, isn't it?"

Old John said, "No, it ain't that bad."

"What do you mean it's not that bad? Why, there goes your henhouse floating downstream right now."

"I know that, but we started raising ducks just a few months ago, and see, there they are, every one of them, just swimming around. Everything is going to be all right."

"Yeah, but man, this high water is going to ruin your crops."

"My crops are already ruined anyhow. It's not going to have any impact. We need a little irrigation. This takes care of that."

As you know, some people persist in being negative. The neighbor said, "Yeah, but look, the water is rising. The first thing you know it's going to be up to your windows."

"Man, I hope it gets there. They're so dirty, they need washing."

We can look at things through two different pairs of eyes: the optimist's eyes or negative eyes. In this chapter, we're going to look at winning through persistence, enthusiasm, and desire.

An old minister was asked why he was so effective. He said, "Well, basically, I tell people what I'm going to tell them. Then I tell them, and then I tell them what I told them." You'll hear me say over and over that repetition is the mother of learning. That makes it the father of action and the architect of accomplishment.

Find Your Front Row Seat

Years ago, I had an opportunity to speak over at Hinds Community College in Raymond, Mississippi, where I had gone to school back in 1943. A man there named Jobie Harris had a profound impact on my life, so I was helping them raise money to establish a scholarship fund honoring him and his wife, Jim El, who also taught there.

The morning I spoke, the auditorium was packed. The students and faculty and visitors from town were standing all the way around the back. As I started, I could not help but notice that there were seven empty seats on the front row and five empty seats in the second row. So I said to the people who were standing, "We have seven empty seats right down here, and five over here. Why don't you come on down and take a comfortable seat for this presentation? All you have to do is walk fifteen or twenty steps, and you're here."

Only one person came down and occupied a seat in the front row. With plenty of front row seats available, only one of them was chosen.

I said to the group, "I wish I were strong enough to pick these seats up, move them to the back, and give them to you, but I'm just not that strong. We don't have that kind of time anyway, and I'm certain the administration would not smile at me doing that. The seats are available, but you have to take the steps to get there.

"In the second row, there are some obstacles you have to overcome, because these five seats happen to be in the middle of the row, but these look like congenial people. They might even help you get past that particular obstacle. That's life itself, because there are always going to be some obstacles that stand between you and what you want, but it's up to you to take the steps."

The point is that front row seats are available, but you have to claim them, and there are some obstacles along the way. You have to climb over those obstacles.

Success versus Ease

We have a tremendous need in America today for front row people, but remember: it's awfully tough to be successful when things are too easy. I'll give you a couple of examples.

Of three hundred world-class leaders—I'm talking about the likes of Churchill, Franklin D. Roosevelt, Helen Keller, Martin Luther King Jr., Mahatma Gandhi—75 percent of them either had been abused as children, had some serious physical disability, or were raised in poverty. It is tough to be successful when things are too easy.

In a motel in Columbia, South Carolina, I met a young man named Fernando Quintero. Fernando is from Mexico. He lived in San Diego for a year and a half. He lived, worked, and associated only with people who spoke Spanish. At the end of a year and a half, he could not speak any English. In his mind, there was no need to.

Then Fernando moved to Columbia, South Carolina. Three months later, he was speaking English; six months later, he was very fluent in the language. He had to, because in Columbia, nobody spoke any Spanish.

My daughter-in-law, who is an extraordinarily bright young woman, is from Campeche, Mexico. She spent a year in New Orleans. All of her friends spoke Spanish. The school was conducted in Spanish. Everything was Spanish. She could not speak any English. Then she came to Austin College, where she met my son. She started the year speaking no English and finished the first year with a 3.0 grade point average. You see, she had to learn it.

A lot of times we don't have people who require us to do things, so if we want to get the most out of life, we have to require those things of ourselves. Life is easier when you're tough on yourself, but life is enormously tough when you're easy on yourself.

The rewards for doing the things I've been talking about are enormous. What does everybody want? To repeat myself, everybody wants to be happy. They want to be healthy. They want to be at least reasonably prosperous. They want to be secure. They want to have friends. They want to have peace of mind. They want to have good family relationships, and they want to have hope.

As I've already pointed out, people wonder whether you can really set happiness as a goal. Rose Barthel says, "Happiness is a conscious choice. It is not an automatic response." Happiness is an attitude. Again, happiness is not a *when* and a *where*. It is a *here* and a *now*.

Many people think they are going to be happy on a *where*: "When we get out to Hawaii for that ten-day vacation, man, then I'm going to be happy." That's not

---

"Happiness is a conscious choice.
It is not an automatic response." —Rose Barthel

the way it is, because it makes no difference where you go; there you are. Until you are happy with *you*, you're not going to be happy with whatever you have or wherever you are.

That doesn't mean that I don't think we ought to have some fun. I love the story about Dallas Theological Seminary. They had a serving line, and at the beginning of the line were apples. There was a little sign that said, "Take only one apple. God is watching." At the end of the line, where they had the chocolate chip cookies, another sign said, "Take as many as you want. God is busy watching the apples."

I believe that we need to have a little fun as we go along, but let's explore happiness a little further and see what we can do about it. I'll ask you to answer these questions in your own mind.

Do you believe that your happiness has anything to do with your health? In other words, if you're healthy and feeling good, will that increase your chances of happiness?

Do you believe that if you were at least prosperous enough that you didn't have to worry about a flat tire or a plumbing foul-up, that could be a contributing factor in being happy?

Do you believe that if you're confident in what you do, secure in the knowledge that your performance will help you keep your job, that too would be a factor in your happiness?

Do you believe that lots of loyal friends will help make you happy? How about peace of mind? If you have that resolved, do you believe that would make you happy?

How about good family relationships? Does your family have anything to do with your happiness?

Now here's the big question. Do you honestly believe that you can do something about your health, your prosperity, your security, your friends, your peace of mind, and good family relationships? Do you believe there's something you can do about it? Won't that give you hope for the future, and isn't it true that hope has something to do with your happiness?

Do you believe, "Yes, there is something I can do about setting happiness as my goal, because it can be a byproduct of all the other things"? Does that make any sense?

I don't know how you feel about that, but when I became really involved in this thinking process, I got enormously excited, because I believe that this is going to represent a breakthrough for many people. Why do I say that? Because certain things also make us unhappy, but when we go down the list, we can say, "I can do something about this," and "I can do something about that."

We can go right back to work to regain what we love. Man, I get excited about that. Let's go down the list and look at the statement that we make so many times: you can have everything in life you want if you'll just help enough other people get what they want. Again, I'm talking philosophy; I'm not talking tactics.

Let me give you a personal example. Many years ago, when I entered the world of selling at the ripe old age of twenty-one, the first two and a half years, we just about starved to death. Things were really tough. Then, thanks to a man named P.C. Merrill, we had a dramatic turnaround. My business exploded. I finished that year the number two salesman out of over seven thousand.

I was in the cookware business. Every year, at the end of August, the company had a National Booster Week. They encouraged every salesperson to pull out all the stops to work eighteen hours a day, make every possible call, give extra bonuses to hostesses, and everything else.

For the first two years, I didn't get excited about Booster Week, because I was struggling to eat, so I couldn't get excited about a lot of other things, but on this particular week, I was primed, and I hit the ground running. I cooked pancakes every morning that week. I prepared a salad every day at lunch for prospects, and I put on a dinner demonstration in the evening.

That week I sold two and a half times as much as I'd ever sold in any week. I tell you, I was motivated. As a matter of fact, I'd sent the redhead and our only daughter down to Jackson, Mississippi, to be with my wife's family because the convention following Booster Week was to be in Biloxi, and I wanted to be able to do nothing but work that week.

In all fairness, the company only encouraged us to maintain that kind of schedule one week out of the year. They explained that, like a rubber band, which is useful only when it's stretched, when you really stretch yourself out sometimes, that's when you can determine your capabilities for doing great things.

I finished making my last call on Saturday night. It was about 10:00. I drove to Atlanta. Bill Cranford, the man who brought me into the business, had said, "Zig, stop by here and catch a few hours' sleep before you drive on."

I woke old Bill up about 2:30 or 3:00 in the morning. He got out of bed and made coffee, and we sat there until 5:30. For those two and half hours, let me tell you what I was doing. I had made thirty-nine sales calls that week and made thirty-four sales. I took Bill Cranford from hello to good-bye for every single one of those experiences. I speak at about 280 words a minute, with gusts up to about 550, so I covered an awful lot of territory.

About 5:30, it suddenly hit me. I said, "Oh, my goodness, Bill. How are you doing?" I had not asked him one single question; I hadn't inquired about his health, his family, his life, his business—nothing. I had totally dominated the conversation. I had the worst case of "I" trouble anybody has ever had. I said, "Bill, I am embarrassed. I apologize."

Bill Cranford said something to me that affected my life and thinking dramatically: "Zig, don't give it a thought. I have thoroughly enjoyed every moment of what you've had to say. Let me remind you, Zig, that I'm the one who brought you in this business. I'm the one who trained you. I'm the one who encouraged you when you were discouraged. I'm the one who took you out in the field and specifically worked with you, holding your hands.

"Zig, until you've experienced what I just experienced, you'll never know what real happiness and real success are. The delight I have received through your success is infinitely greater than the delight you're experiencing by having that success."

The man was 100 percent right. Was he a happy man? You absolutely can count on it. He was a happy man.

Prosperity

Let's look at this thing called prosperity. When I was a boy, I worked in a grocery store down in Yazoo City, Mississippi. It was during the Depression. We had very limited inventories, and 90 percent of all of the business that was done in that store was done from 4:00 Friday afternoon until 11:00 on Saturday night. That's when everybody got paid. Merchants carried very limited inventories. We frequently ran out of what we were selling, and we borrowed from the other merchants.

There was a young man named Charlie Scott who worked across the street. He was their runner for that store, as I was a runner for the store I worked in.

Many times Charlie would hit our front door in a dead run, and he would say to our owner, "Mr. Anderson, I need to borrow a half dozen cans of tomatoes."

Mr. Anderson would say, "Charlie, you know where they are. Go get them." Old Charlie, in a dead run, would go back to the shelf where the tomatoes were, scoop up six cans, run back up to the counter, plop them down, sign his name indicating he'd gotten them, and scoot out the front door.

One day, I asked Mr. Anderson, "Why on earth does Charlie Scott always run everywhere?"

Mr. Anderson grinned kindly and said, "Charlie's working for a raise, and he's going to get it too."

"Mr. Anderson, how do you know Charlie Scott is going to get a raise?"

"I know Charlie Scott is going to get a raise because if the man he's working for doesn't give it to him, I am."

That's employment security. Regardless of who signs the check, you work for yourself, and when you make that big effort, things are going to happen.

A few years ago, speaking at Mississippi State University, I told that story. When it was over, a tall, slender fellow came up to me and said, "Let me ask you. When is the last time you've seen Charlie Scott?"

"Well," I said, "Charlie is two years older than I am. That means he left Yazoo City in 1942 to go into the service. I haven't seen him since then."

"You probably wouldn't even recognize him, would you?"

"No, I wouldn't."

"I didn't think so. I'm Charlie Scott."

Charlie Scott retired at age fifty. He was successful in every area of his life, because he took those habits he had acquired in childhood, which was a tough one, and applied them all of his life, and he was able to accomplish the objectives that I'm talking about.

Security determines the way you handle situations in life, particularly in your relationships. I love the story about an experience that the Buddha had.

A man met him on the street one day and began to call him mean and ugly names. The Buddha listened quietly and thoughtfully until the man ran out of epithets and had to pause for breath.

"If you offer something to a man, and he refuses it, to whom does it belong?" asked the Buddha.

The spiteful man replied, "It belongs, I suppose, to the one who offered it."

Then the Buddha said, "The abuse and vile names you offer me I refuse to accept." The detractor turned and walked away.

A secure individual is never made to feel inferior by the insecure people of life, the faultfinders and backbiters, the ne'er-do-wells, the critics. Being secure within ourselves is really what matters.

How do you determine what makes a person secure? You're what you are and where you are because of what's gone into your mind. You change what you are and where you are by changing what goes into your mind.

How do you get friends? The best way to get friends is to be a friend. Most people who go out in life looking for friends will find them scarce, but when you go out in life to be a friend, you'll find them everywhere. The Bill Cranford attitude will enable people to have more friends.

What is peace of mind? I have great respect for a young man named Peter Lowe, who does seminars that I speak at all over the country. Peter was going to buy his mother-in-law a little business. As he analyzed these businesses, in twenty-two straight instances, he would ask them if they had another set of books, and all twenty-two responded, "Yes, I do."

Peter would look at that other set of books, and he said, "You know, Zig, the sad thing is the amount they were stealing from the government was very little—$1,000, $5,000—but can you imagine the grief and turmoil they go through every time an official-looking agent comes walking in and announces, 'I'm from the government, and I'm here to help.'"

You know exactly what I'm talking about. Do these individuals have peace of mind? How much

---

"You are what you are and where you are because
of what's gone into your mind. You can change
what you are and where you are by changing
what goes into your mind." —Zig Ziglar

more productive would they have been had they played it straight and were able to utilize all of their creative resources? I believe it would make a dramatic difference.

For me, peace of mind comes when I understand where I will spend eternity. I was excited to read recently that 90 percent of the people in America believe in God. Now if we can persuade them to believe in God, then we really will have something to be excited about.

Good family relationships are enormously important, as is hope. If you have all of these things, your hope can be absolutely legitimate. Hope is the fuel that propels the engine of effort through the difficult times and over the obstacles which regularly appear on the roadway to success.

All of these things constitute a package. If you want these things, you must plan for them. Total success demands responsibility—responsibility for your conduct and your performance, because all of these have consequences.

I love this little bit by Robert Orbin along these lines: Two parents were comparing notes. One said, "I'm really concerned. Our kids are getting into so much trouble. I don't think the daycare center, nursery school, after-school program, and babysitters are raising them right."

That really does say something, doesn't it? Responsibility is what I'm talking about.

Understand something: winners don't always finish first. You see, there's a confused belief in our society that unless you are the absolute best and you win every time, you're not a winner. But winners do not always finish first. Winners give best effort.

In one Super Bowl, one of the real winners was a member of the Buffalo Bills football team. It was a blowout. The Dallas Cowboys beat them 52 to 17, and everybody knows that I'm a dyed-in-the-wool Cowboys fan.

Had you been born and raised in communist China, you today would be a communist. Had you been raised in the jungle somewhere where they practice voodoo and worship idols, you probably would have been an idol worshiper, but if you were born and raised in Dallas, you're going to grow up believing in the Dallas Cowboys.

In any case, it's toward the end of the game; we're leading 52 to 17. There's a fumble that hits the ground and bounces up. Leon Lett of the Cowboys grabs that ball and lumbers toward the end zone. He gets within twenty yards, and I watched the replay to make absolutely certain that I had my yardage right.

When Leon Lett was on the ten-yard line, he started hotdogging it big-time, prancing over, holding his football out there. When Leon was on the ten-yard line, Don Beebe, the outstanding wide receiver for the Buffalo Bills, was on the twenty-yard line. He made up ten yards on Leon in less than it took Leon to make that twenty yards, and he slapped the ball away. We did not get the touchdown.

Understand that there was no way on earth—and Don Beebe knew that—that the Bills had a chance to win that game, but effort, personal pride, everything was at stake as far as Don was concerned. Coincidentally, it's his doing that helped his team to avoid the biggest loss ever in Super Bowl history.

What am I saying? You win when you give it your best effort.

Dropping the Ball

A lot of times in life, things happen over which we have no control. In 1986, Penn State and Notre Dame were playing, and Penn State was ahead. Notre Dame had the ball. They were driving down to the end of the field. Their tight end got loose in the end zone. The quarterback hit him letter-perfect right in the hands. He dropped the ball. Had he caught the ball, Notre Dame would have won. He dropped the ball, Penn State won, and went on to win the national championship.

Here's the message. Ten players on the Notre Dame team had done everything they were supposed to. They had filled their assignment to perfection, but one person dropped the ball.

I don't care what your job is. I don't care how circumstances are with you, in your home, in your school, in your job, or in the factory. On a number of occasions you're going to do everything you're sup-posed to, and somebody else is going to drop the ball.

We have to learn to deal with the dropped balls of life. Our attitude, our self-image really does make the difference. The question is, do we respond to life, or do we react to it? As you know, responding is posi-tive; reacting is negative.

Success absolutely demands change, and it demands creativity. Many people resist that change.

One of my favorite stories is about the fellow who won a bass fiddle in a contest. The instruction book had all the pages torn out except page one, and all it showed was how to have your left hand up on the neck and your right hand on the bow. He fig-ured that was the way to play a bass fiddle, so that's the way he was playing. Johnny One-Note—that was him.

It drove his wife crazy in short order. Then she hit the jackpot. Somebody gave her a ticket to the sym-phony. She came down and got right there next to the stage—as luck would have it, next to the bass fiddle player.

When she got home that evening, she was excited. She said, "I was sitting next to the guy playing the bass fiddle, almost underneath him, and I noticed

---

We have to learn to deal with the "dropped balls" of life. Our attitude and our self-image really does make the difference.

---

that he kept moving his left hand up and down, and he kept moving the bow all over the place, and I can't help but notice that you keep yours on exactly the same spot. Why is that?"

That old boy never broke stride. He said, "That's easy to explain. That fellow is still looking for his place in life. I done found mine."

If you've already found you really want everything in life, maybe you don't want to read this, but the fact that you are reading it tells me beyond any doubt that you are open to that change.

Motivation + Information = Inspiration

Let me say here that motivation plus information equals inspiration. A woman named Mary Ellen Caldwell was at a seminar of mine. During one of the breaks, she came up to me and said, "Look what I've got."

She showed me a list of things that she was going to be doing to encourage her dad, who had been forced into retirement against his will at age sixty-five. She said, "Dad really has lost heart. He's not excited about life. He's frustrated. He doesn't feel there's any use for him. Look, you've given me all of these ideas."

In fact I had not talked about retirement and had not given her any ideas at all. Then what on earth happened? Let me describe it exactly, because I believe this is the key to many of the mysteries of life;

it explains why people so often fail to do more with their lives.

Number one, Mary Ellen had taken her lifetime of information and experience. Understand that she'd learned a great deal.

As an aside, let me give you an intriguing bit of information. This is subjective; I don't know how on earth you could possibly prove it, but I believe it has validity. Two of the most brilliant PhDs I've ever known in my life have told me this: in your lifetime of experience, if you have your PhD, less than one-half of 1 percent of your total knowledge inventory came from a formal educational environment. Now don't misunderstand me: I'm not saying education is not important. The first thing you do is you learn to read, and then you read to learn, but later, you learn to read people as well.

In any case, Mary Ellen had had a tremendous number of life experiences. That's number one. Second, she had a love and a concern for her dad. Third, she was involved in this personal growth seminar.

Let's see if we can cast some light on what happened. Motivation, you see, is the spark that lights the fire of knowledge. Let me also say that the more you already know and the broader your base is, the more new ideas and information will benefit you. In order to put all of this to work, you need to take some quiet time to put it all together.

A friend of mine named Fred Smith, whom I've identified as my mentor, was having dinner with my wife and me once. As always, I had my notepad with me. I never see him without carrying a notepad. He always puts something heavy on me.

That night he said one thing that got me excited: "Zig, remember that great learners are not always great thinkers." I got to reflecting on that. I was in Tampa, Florida, and I'd been in a dental chair for about five hours that day, and I decided I wasn't going to do my exercise, but I wanted to go for a stroll.

I had a very casual forty-minute walk followed by a very quiet dinner. I got to reflecting on this thing called motivation, and to motivate is to pull out or draw out that which is on the inside. Motivation plus information equals inspiration. Then suddenly things came together. It explained what had happened to Mary Ellen Caldwell, and it explains what happens to us every day of our lives.

Mary Ellen took the information which she'd accumulated over a long period of time. I gave her some brand-new information, which got her excited, and then up popped some information she thought she'd forgotten about because she hadn't used it. Up popped that information, and up popped the information that I'd just given her. They took a look at each other, this information and that information, and they said, "Hey, I like you. Do you like me?" "Yeah, let's get together." A marriage service was performed, and a birth of completely brand-new ideas took place.

In addition to all the information we get, there are times when we absolutely must be quiet. We have to be thinking about what we're dealing with. When we do, it's amazing what will happen. You regularly need the motivational input that brings in new information, which stirs up the old information. Both of them come to the front and get together, and that's what creates new ideas.

As valuable as motivational recordings are, there are occasions when you do not want to have them or anything else on. For example, when you're walking, instead of listening to music or motivational lectures, think about your business or something you're wrestling with. It's amazing how many times brand-new ideas will be born to you.

As I was talking, because of the motivation, Mary Ellen brought out things she thought she had forgotten. Motivation is to pull out or draw out. She took the new information, and that is exactly what happened.

How to Use Creativity

How can we use creativity in any area of life? Let me share with you one of the most exciting letters that I've ever gotten. It's from a man named Carl Hugebeck. He teaches character education in the "I Can" course down in Bastrop, Texas. He had just finished a class, and here's what he said:

"These kids are at-risk. I reminded them that because they live in the United States of America, lifelong education and self-improvement are a reality. These students have had difficult backgrounds and live in some very poor situations. They are not supposed to be optimistic, enthusiastic, and goal-oriented. They are. I tell them that they are at-risk. If they keep doing what they're doing, they will be at risk of graduating, going to college, meeting their ideal mate, prospering, and enjoying the type of life God intended them to have. So, yes, thanks to character education and I Can, our students really are at-risk."

Don't you just love that little twist? Think of all the students who have been told over and over, "You're at-risk. You've been victim of this, that and the other." Of course, in many cases it's true: they have been victims.

But it makes more sense to use creative imagination and say, "If you keep doing this, you're at risk of graduating. You're at risk of getting a promotion. You're at risk of being successful. You're at risk of having lots of friends." Creativity makes a difference.

Let me give you another example here. Walter Williams happens to be one of my favorite economists. He once had an editorial in the *Dallas Morning News.*

He says here, "Anyim Palmer founded the Marcus Garvey School in South Central LA in '75. If you visit it, you would see two-year-olds reciting the ABCs, three-year-olds counting in English, Spanish, and Swahili, and four-year-olds doing math. Down the hall, you would see second-graders spelling words like *pharmaceutical, entrepreneur,* and *cerebellum* and repeating verbatim from memory 'The Gettysburg Address.'"

What kind of school is this? It's not a rich, white suburban school. It is a black school with four hundred students, located in a troubled section of Los Angeles. Its students are not gifted. They're ordinary kids with concerned parents.

The administrators and teachers, who are also black, have unbounded pride and a sense of mission. Are the teachers real experts? No. They're regular teachers. As a matter of fact, they don't even have teaching credentials. What makes them so unique? They're given the freedom to adjust and be held accountable to teach the students the most effective things for their needs.

Again, with creativity, we can do an awful lot more things.

Drugs, Crime, and Alcohol

Why did I mention something like "I Can"? Why did I talk about what's happening in a school? It's very simple. Every one of us, you and me is involved in drugs, crime, gangs, and alcohol—the whole schmear.

My son's best friend was killed by a drunken teenager doing ninety miles an hour through a red light one night about midnight.

My brother-in-law had his home broken into by a drug addict, who stole an heirloom picture. An hour later, that picture was in the addict's veins in the form of heroin.

I check into a luxury hotel. They give me a key to room 2165 and say, "But the key says you're in 1710."

"What's the deal?" I say.

"In case you're mugged, they won't know where to come to get the rest of your stuff."

I pull up to a service station at 9:00 at night, and a sign says, "Please pay before you pump the gas." We do not live in a low-rent neighborhood, but there's only one street my wife is comfortable walking on in broad daylight.

We are all victims of these problems, so we need to get involved in the solutions. Where does it start? Obviously with you.

Now I'm going to share a little bit of information here. I'm enormously excited about it, because a lot of people in our society have behavior which is uncharacteristic or which we cannot even begin to understand.

I got a letter from a gentleman down in Florida named Leland M. Heller, MD. He talks about borderline disorder, which affects between 4 and 8 percent of the population. He says that borderline disorder . . .

> . . . is one of the major preventable causes of child abuse, divorces, substance abuse, and impulsive violent crimes. It's a very important topic, and a treatable illness.
>
> It's basically a form of epilepsy in the brain's limbic system. Victims have abnormal neurolog-

*ical examinations, brain waves, memory, and
sleep. Borderline is clearly a medical problem,
but it's also an emotional problem. Borderlines
have no self-esteem, no effective psychological
defenses, and have spent a lifetime with crip-
pling mood swings, horribly painful dysphoria,
and frequent bouts of psychosis, and have dis-
torted their understanding of life and people.*

Until the proper medication came along, people
with borderline disorder had essentially no chance
to recover, even with counseling. (This is where we
need to understand people a little better.) Dr. Heller
points out that somewhere between 7 million and 20
million people in this country suffer from this disorder. Now where does this fit in your life?

Dr. Heller adds, "In my opinion, it is unlikely a
borderline will ever achieve mental wellness without reading positive books."

Motivational books are a must. They are as
important as the drugs. You need the right information in order to change the way you think and feel.

I once had a conversation with Dr. Les Carter,
who's on the staff at Minirth-Meier Clinic. I said, "I
have an idea. Let me check it out and see what you
think about it. In my opinion, the purpose of all
counseling is to change your thinking."

"Zig," he said, "you're 100 percent on the target."

Changing the thinking of these people is making a dramatic difference. Dr. Carter had some nice

things to say about me: "Zig is not only funny and motivational, but he describes values and attitudes that improves one's chances for a successful life. Untreated borderlines have shifting values due to their illness." That happens to a lot of us, doesn't it? Shifting values. "Zig gives a set of values borderlines and the rest of us can believe in and live by. You may disagree with some things. Not everyone agrees on everything Zig says, especially religion, but you will find few areas of disagreement. I greatly admire what his tapes have done for my patients."

I recognize that that sounds a little self-serving. Please forgive me if it does, but it's meant to say that when you have the right input, when the input is good and clean and pure and positive, what has happened in the past absolutely can change. You change the future by changing your thinking. You change your thinking by putting the right things in your mind.

Role Models

You'll probably agree with me that role models are enormously important. Do you believe that a role model's lifestyle will have an effect on the lifestyle of the person who emulates that model?

Let me identify the role models for the children in America who are between the ages of seven and twelve. For 39 percent of them, their number one hero is a movie star or television star; for 19 percent, their hero is a singer (and in virtually every case, you can read that as a rock or rap singer); for 11 percent of them, their number one hero is a comedian; and for 11 percent, their number one hero is an athlete.

I'm not putting down those people, but how many of them would you want your child to be like? To emulate? To follow their habits, their patterns?

We need to look at what we are putting in our minds, because, you see, a major business in today's world is counseling.

I also asked Dr. Carter, "What percentage of counseling has to do with relationships?"

He said, "100 percent of all counseling has to do directly or indirectly with the relationships of one kind or another."

What's the most important relationship of all? That relationship you have with yourself. When you get along with *you*, it's easier to get along with somebody else.

In one recent survey, when managers were asked what trait they most desired in employees, 84 percent of them said, "I want somebody who can get along, be a part of the team, work with, and cooperate with the rest of us."

Have you noticed that when you have one wet blanket in the crowd, it puts a damper on the rest? If you get one negative person talking, it catches on. That why the managers say they want people who can get along with others.

The Roman emperor and philosopher Marcus Aurelius said, "The happiness of your life depends upon the quality of your thoughts." What affects your thoughts? What goes in your mind? As I've said, your associates also affect your thoughts.

Now let me say that the principles that we're talking about work for individuals, they work for schools, they work for businesses, and they work for nations. I say "principles" rather than "procedures," because when you try to get everybody following the same procedure, you tend to have problems. That stifles creativity. Nevertheless, you start with a base to build on, and that's what I'm talking about when I say "principles."

You change the future by changing your thinking.
You can change your thinking by putting the
right things in your mind.

Chapter 5
The Bernie Lofchick Story

I want to share with you a story which I believe represents our philosophy as well as any I've ever heard. As you read it, I believe you're going to think that it ought to give anybody hope that they can do things in their life.

In 1965, I was speaking in Kansas City. It was my first major presentation. On the program were Elmer Wheeler ("The World's Greatest Statesman"), educator Dr. Kenneth McFarland, Senator Milward Simpson, and management expert Joe Batten. It was a bunch of heavy hitters; I was the new kid on the block.

I felt somewhat like the farmer who entered his mule in the Kentucky Derby. Somebody asked him, "You don't really think that mule is going to win that derby, do you?"

"Man, no," he said. "No way."

"Why on earth would you enter him?"

"I just figured the association would be good for him."

Anyway, when the seminar finished that evening, I headed back over to the Muehlebach Hotel for what I thought was going to be a lonely dinner. I stepped out of the elevator, and I heard the booming voice of a man whom I now love as one of my closest friends; he's really more like a brother. His name is Bernie Lofchick. He said, "Zig, where are you going?"

"I'm going to dinner."

"Come with me, and I'll buy."

That's an offer that's hard to refuse. As you know, people are happy when they can do things for you, and I liked to make him happy, so I said, "Brother Bern, you have a deal."

We sat down to dinner. Do you know how some people establish rapport instantly? We're both from large families. His dad died when he was young. He worked in a grocery story early on; I worked in a grocery store. He was running the biggest cookware company in Canada; I'd sold cookware. So we had a lot in common, and I said, "Bernie, did you fly all the way down from Winnipeg to attend this seminar?"

"Yes, and was it ever worth it. I got some great ideas."

"But, Bernie, to come down from Winnipeg to here—that cost you a whole lot of money." I can't believe I was that negative.

"Yes, Zig, but thanks to my son, David, money is no problem for me."

"Brother Bern, that sounds like a story. Tell me."

"When David was born, our joy was absolute and complete. We already had our two daughters, and now we had our son. But very quickly we came to realize that something was wrong. His little head hung too limply to the right side of his body. He drooled too much to be a normal, healthy child. We took him to the doctor, and he said it was no problem, he was going to outgrow it, but deep down we knew something was wrong.

"We took him to a specialist, one of the most respected ones in Canada, who said he just had club feet. For about six weeks they treated him for that, but we knew it was more serious. We took him to yet another specialist. After a very comprehensive examination, the specialist said, 'This little boy is a spastic. He has cerebral palsy. He's never going to be able to walk or talk or count to ten. I encourage you to put him in an institution for his own good and for the good of the other members of the family.'"

Bernie Lofchick has the most vivid eyes I've ever seen in my life. Those dark eyes were flashing as he said, "But, Zig, I'm not a buyer. I'm a seller. I could not see my son as a helpless, hopeless vegetable all of his life. I saw my son"—and here's the visualization I've been talking about—"I saw my son as a happy, healthy, productive individual. So we went to another specialist and another and another. Over twenty specialists said there is no hope for this boy. Then we heard of a Dr. Perlstein down in Chicago, who was reputed to be the number one authority in the world on cerebral palsy, but he was so busy we could not get an appointment for the next two years."

Bernie is a salesman. He made some calls and used some connections. He learned that Dr. Perlstein was a bridge player, playing with his son every Friday night. He got the son's phone number. He called and talked to Dr. Perlstein on the phone, and arranged that when they had the first cancellation, they would call Bernie and Elaine, who would bring David down to Chicago for the exam.

About eleven days later, the call came through. A little boy from Australia had canceled. They took David to Chicago. When the examination was over, Dr. Perlstein called the Lofchicks in and said to them, "Your little boy is a spastic. He has cerebral palsy. He's never going to be able to walk or talk or count to ten if you listen to the prophets of doom, but I want you to know that I am not problem-conscious; I am solution-conscious. I believe there is something you can do for your son if you're willing to do your part."

The Lofchicks said, "Doctor, we will do anything. Name the price." At that point in his career, they could not afford a heavy financial burden.

Dr. Perlstein said, and he and his nurses spelled it out in minute detail. "It is going to cost an awful lot of money, but far more importantly, it's going to take an awful lot of commitment and patience and discipline on your part. You're going to have to push this little boy beyond all human endurance. Then you're going to have to push him some more.

"You're going to have to work him until he falls; then you need to pick him up and work him some more. You need to understand that there's going to be months, sometimes years, when you cannot visually see any progress at all, but you cannot stop. You have to keep going. Otherwise he goes all the way back.

"One other thing. Don't ever let him take therapy where he can physically see another victim of cerebral palsy taking therapy, because instinctively and subconsciously they will pick up the awkward, inadvertent moves that they sometimes make. Make certain there's a screen so he does not see those things."

When Bernie and Elaine headed back to Winnipeg, Canada, for the first time in their son's life, they had hope, and hope, you know, is so incredibly important. They felt that the Goliath of cerebral palsy now had an opponent with a legitimate chance to win this battle.

The Lofchicks hired a physical therapist and a bodybuilder, and they went to work. It took many months for David even to move the length of his own body. It took him many more months before the therapist called Bernie in his office one day and said, "Come on home, Bernie. I believe David is ready for the supreme effort."

Bernie rushed home and went down to the little gymnasium they had built in the basement. The therapist and the bodybuilder, several of the neighbors, the two big sisters, everybody was around David on that little mat. He was going to attempt to do a push-up.

As he rose into the air, the physical and emotional exertion was so great that his body was covered with perspiration. The mat looked as if somebody had sprinkled water on it. It was an effort that we cannot conceive of today, but when that perfect push-up was completed, David and Mom and Dad, the therapist, the bodybuilder, and the neighbors all broke down and wept. They were the tears that clearly say happiness is not pleasure; happiness is victory.

One of the highlights of our life took place on October 23, 1971, when we flew to Winnipeg to attend the bar mitzvah of little David Lofchick. As that boy walked tall and straight and strong to the front of the synagogue to take part in the ceremony that would move him into the manhood of his faith, his only concession to the disease was a dragging of the right foot, which was so slight you had to know about it in advance to even have seen it.

At that time, David had run as much as five miles nonstop, had done up to a thousand push-ups in a single day. He was running the wheels off of his third bicycle. David was skating on the neighborhood hockey team. What's so amazing about all of that is they had said, "Your boy has no motor connection to the right side of his body. He will never be able to swim. He will never be able to skate. He will never be able to ride a bicycle."

I give you all these details because I believe it's one of the most moving, most inspiring, most important stories that I have ever been privileged to participate in.

Dr. Ken McFarland, former superintendent of education in Topeka, Kansas, was one of my heroes and one of the greatest speakers I've ever heard. When he was a little guy in school, his teacher asked him, "Ken, how far do you want to go in life?"

"As far as I can," Ken said.

Then she pointed to the floor and said, "Ken, the ladder starts here." The foundation is so incredibly important.

Learning from the Lofchicks

Let's take a serious look at the David Lofchick story to see the lessons that we can learn.

First of all, let's look at the foundation stone of honesty. When times are tough, when you really have a difficult assignment in front of you, honesty is an absolute must. To tell somebody what they want to hear today, knowing that it's going to come back and bite you tomorrow, is destructive.

David's doctors and therapists and family were honest with him: "This is going to keep going a long time." They prepared him for the long haul. Honesty is a tremendously important foundation stone to build on.

What is character? It's the ability to carry out a good resolution long after the excitement of the moment has passed. When we set long-term goals, character is what's going to enable us to reach them, because there will be times when we will absolutely want to quit. We wonder, is it really worth it?

If you were to see David Lofchick today, you would say yes, it really is worth it. David has three beautiful children. The only concession he makes to the disease is, again, so minute that you could not even identify it unless you knew about it.

He's an entrepreneur and has been enormously successful in the real estate business. He worked with his dad in one of the largest Maytag distributorships in the world. He has now opened his own computer store. He has a lot of things going for him.

Was it worth it? Absolutely, a thousand times yes, it was worth it. His success is built on integrity. With integrity, you have nothing to fear because you have nothing to hide.

This story is also built on love; it's one of the most beautiful love stories I've ever heard. When David was about eighteen months old, they had to put braces on his little legs, and every night when they put them on, they had to progressively make them tighter and tighter.

David was a beautiful little boy, with green eyes, an olive complexion, coal-black hair, and every night

---

What is character? It is the ability to carry out a
good resolution long after the moment has passed.

---

he would look at his mom or his dad. He would say to them, "Do you have to put them on tonight? Do you have to make them so tight?"

I don't think there's a parent who will ever read this who cannot relate to what I'm saying. Your child, your baby, the one you love, with tears in his eyes, is saying, "Can't we leave them off tonight?" or "Do you have to make them so tight?"

David's parents loved him so much that they were willing to say no to the tears of the moment in order to say yes to the healthy laughter of a lifetime.

Loving someone doesn't mean you always give them what they think they want at that moment. Loving someone is doing for that person what is best for that person at that moment. That's what love is all about.

From the loyalty of Bernie's family to David, the loyalty of all of his relatives, of his sisters, of the therapist and the bodybuilder, they became an extremely close family. Often serious illnesses split families apart. This one brought that family closer together.

Loyalty and Success

How does this apply in the business world? How does loyalty fit into our own success?

One afternoon years ago, when I was writing at my home, the doorbell rang. I went to the door. It was a good friend of mine named Bryan Flanagan, who also worked with us. Bryan was a little pensive, a little hesitant as he came in. He said, "You know, I hate to interrupt what you're doing, but I just got some news and wanted to tell you personally."

He'd come to tell me that he was leaving the company. He said, "Let me tell you about an offer I have, Zig; I'm enormously excited about it." He started describing it, and I got excited about it too.

"Bryan," I said, "I hate to see you go. I really do." He was a very valuable member of our staff, but he left with my blessings.

He came back a few months later and said, "Everything that glitters is not gold. I would like to come back and work with you again." We were, of course, elated to have him back.

But let me tell you why he got the offer that he got in the first place. Everywhere Bryan went, he talked about what a great company he worked for and what a fine person I was. He was bragging about all of us. He was saying, "It's a great place to work. The attitude is so great. Everybody tries to live like they say they do. It's a wonderful place to work."

Now let me ask you a question. Do you think Bryan would have gotten any job offer or opportunity from anybody else if everywhere he went he'd said, "You can't beat that lousy, no good outfit I work for. They're a bunch of bums. They tell you one thing and do another thing. I can't understand anybody acting like they do." How many employers would have said, "That sounds like the kind of the guy I'd like to have working for me"?

What I'm talking about here is absolutely practical in every area of life.

Character and Difficulty

The person of character finds a special attractiveness in difficulty, because it is only through coming to grips with difficulty that a person can realize his or her potentialities. I have wondered how much bigger, stronger, faster, and smarter David would have been had he been given all of the chances at birth that you and I were given.

Then one day it hit me. Had he been given more, in all probability he would have ended up with less, maybe considerably less. That's one of the reasons I take refuge in my faith so often. The scripture says that all things work together for good. We're supposed to thank God for difficulties. The more I delve into my research, the more I become convinced that we develop strengths by overcoming the difficulties of life.

The person of character finds a special attractiveness in difficulty, because it is only through coming to grips with difficulty that a person can realize his or her potentialities.

Building Self-Image

Let's look at another thing. David Lofchick, in the beginning, could not have a healthy self-image, but author Dr. Tony Campolo says the most important person in your life influences your self-image more than anything else.

Who were the most important person or persons in David's life? His parents. What did they do to reinforce that image? Every night, when he was a baby until he got to be a teenager, Bernie Lofchick would come in. He worked in the evening at a housewares company. For seven years, Bernie Lofchick worked seven days and seven nights a week. He took one Friday night off in seven years because of the enormity of the expenses that went with giving David this chance in life. In the process, he became the largest housewares distributor in Canada, and he got there simply because he was helping his son get what he wanted out of life. Was it tough? It sure was.

But every night when Bernie would come in, David would be asleep. He would awaken him, and he'd hold him in his arms, and he would say, "Son, I love you very much, and I want you to know that you can do anything you really want to do, son. You are a winner in every sense of the word." Bernie's wife, Elaine, had already told David that before he went to sleep the first time. Over and over, the love was total, it was unconditional, and he grew up with that security.

Security, your self-image, is enormously important. It begins with having the right attitude—towards yourself, your fellow human beings, your job, the company you work with, the community you live in, the country of which we're a part.

Chapter 6
The Power of Principles

I would like to emphasize how these principles work in your personal life, your family life, in your business life, and yes, nationally.

You've heard a lot about W. Edwards Deming, the man who revolutionized the Japanese system of doing things. Homer Sarasohn was another management guru who went over there and did a tremendous job for them, but let me tell you why they were able to do the things they did.

Here's a little nation half the size of the State of Texas. Two-thirds of the land cannot be used for anything. They have no natural resources, no oil, no gas, no coal, no iron ore—none of those things, only half as many people as we have, and yet they're one of the leading nations in the world.

That's because they have developed the most important resource of all. It ties into what Supreme Court judge Oliver Wendell Holmes Jr. said: "The great tragedy in America is not the waste of our natural resources, though that is great. The great tragedy is the waste of our human resources, because the average person goes to their grave with their music still in them."

It's a cliché, but you know it's true. You're the only one who can use your ability. It is an awesome responsibility.

Why were the Japanese able to do so much? It was because of what General Douglas MacArthur did. After Japan was defeated in World War II, MacArthur oversaw the American occupation. He knew that ever since 1853, when Commodore Perry opened the doors of Japan, it had been a warlike nation. When he came in to rewrite the Japanese constitution, he knew that he could not change a warlike nation overnight into a peaceful, producing nation. He knew he had to start at the very base—with the children—so he brought in an educator, Dr. Mark T. Orr. Dr. Orr was brought in to completely revise the Japanese educational structure in Japan.

Dr. Bill Kirby, who was the commissioner of education here in the State of Texas, went to Japan and did a study on the Japanese educational system. Here's what they learned. In Japan, in kindergarten, one hour a day, every day, they teach a course emphasizing the values of honesty, character, integrity, hard work, loyalty, thrift, enthusiasm, positive thinking, responsibility, patriotism, and free enterprise. What we have been talking about during this entire series.

There is a relationship and cooperation between the parent and the student and between the educator, the government, and the businesspeople; they work together. They turned out a workforce that was ready to go to work. That's what I'm talking about here: developing a workforce built on the principles that we've been talking about.

At the Thomas Jefferson Center in Pasadena, California, they spent years studying values worldwide, and here's what they found: there are fifteen values that are common in all the world's great civilizations and religions. Number one is wisdom, number two is integrity, three is love, four is freedom; that's where creativity is born. Five is justice, six is courage, seven is humility, eight is patience, nine is industriousness, ten is thrift, eleven is generosity, twelve is objectivity, thirteen is cooperation, fourteen is moderation, and fifteen is optimism. All of these are the qualities that I've been talking about.

Ronald Reagan, got right to the heart of it: "If we fail to instruct our children in justice, religion, and liberty, we will be condemning them to a world without virtue, a life in the twilight of a civilization where the great truths have been forgotten." I believe he's right.

"If we fail to instruct our children in justice, religion, and liberty, we will be condemning to a world without virtue, a life in the twilight of civilization where the great truths have been forgotten." —President Ronald Reagan.

Attitude can be good today and bad tomorrow. We know how things happen to us, and we react instead of responding, and so our attitude is subject to a lot of things.

Daniel Goleman had an interesting article in *The New York Times*. Again, this ties into the David Lofchick story. Most importantly, it ties into your story and your life.

A study of more than 2,800 men and women sixty-five and older found that those who rate their health as poor are forty-five times more likely to die in the next four years than those who rate their health as excellent. This was the case even if examinations showed the respondents to be in comparable health.

One group saw themselves negatively; the other saw themselves positively. You're drawn closest to the strongest picture in your mind, and the results, in this case, were fatal. These findings are supported by a review of five other large studies totaling 23,000 people. In other words, it was a big study.

The old saying, "As a man thinketh in his heart, so is he," has a great deal of validity. Whether you think you can or think you can't, you're absolutely right.

When Bernie Lofchick got the news that his son was a spastic and would be a vegetable, he immediately said, "I don't buy that idea. I see my son as living a happy, healthy, normal life."

Faith is also involved in a situation like that. I love the story of the fellow who stopped at the mountain overlook to get a better view of the scenery. He got a little too close to the edge, it collapsed under him, and he started falling. It was about a four-hundred-foot drop. He caught on to the last remaining little tree that was sticking out, and he started shouting for help.

There was a deep voice: "Son, do you believe?"

"Oh, yes, I believe. I believe."

"Let go of the limb."

"Is there anybody else up there?"

As you know, a lot of people are unfortunately too often in that mode of faith.

The Stairway of Relationships

You can think of building relationships as a stairway to the top. At the top, we look at what you want. At the bottom, we look at the foundation, and then we take the steps in order to get there. The elevator to the top is out of order. It always has been. You're going to have to take the stairs, and you're going to have to take them one at a time.

As for family relationships, let me make a little confession to you. I have three daughters and a son.

There's never been a doubt in my mind that I loved each of my children equally, but as my son grew into a man, he got married, and went into business for himself, I started noticing something. I never would have noticed it had I not heard what former NFL player and inspirational speaker Bill Glass had to say: "I never see one of my girls and I never talk to them on the telephone without, somewhere in the conversation, telling them how much I love them."

I love my boy fully as much as I do my girls, but over the years, I'd gotten away from telling him that. Sometimes we men don't do those things. I heard Bill Glass talk about an experience with his 285-pound son and how he hugged him and said, "Son, I sure love you."

His son said, "Thanks, Dad. I needed that." Everybody needs that.

The sad thing is that many of us love our family a great deal, but somehow or another we expect them to figure it out by osmosis. But it needs to be verbalized.

A few days after I'd heard Bill Glass, my son and I had a round of golf, which is our favorite recreational activity. We got back to the house. We were moving the clubs from my car over to his, and I said, "Son, I have a confession to make to you. I've noticed over a period of time that I'm neglecting something which is extraordinarily important. I have just about quit telling you how much I love you. I want you to know, son, that I do love you."

My son said, "Dad, I know that," but there was a just a trace of a tear. He grabbed me, and he hugged me, and ever since then, when we greet each other, it's no longer with a handshake. He gives me a hug.

I can't say it strongly enough. Dad, it's so important that you love your son. I don't care if he's twenty-eight or sixty-five. You need to hug that son of yours. I know you're going to hug your girls, but you need to hug your boy and tell him that you love him. That makes all the difference in the world. I believe that is one of the prime reasons David Lofchick has done so well: he was given that reassurance over and over.

The Power of Small Objectives

You need a series of goals in life, and sometimes when the goal is so far off, we may lose sight of the final objective unless we have daily objectives along the way.

One of my favorite people is Byron Nelson. I bring this example in because it supports exactly what I'm talking about. In 1944 Byron won eight golf tournaments and made $38,000. That was a lot of money on the golf tour in those days. It was a lot of money in life in those days. That got him set for 1945.

In 1945, Byron set a record that will never be broken. I emphatically believe that: nobody will ever approach the record he set in 1945. He won 11 consecutive golf tournaments. He entered 31 tournaments and won a total of 18 before the year was over. He placed second 7 times, so 25 out of 31 times he did no worse than second. The worst he ever finished was ninth.

What set up 1945 was 1944. What sets up a winner over here is what you do before you get there. Winning those tournaments in 1944 set the stage, but let me tell you what was really responsible.

Byron was keeping exact records. He said, "I was so consistent in my game that I could hit the fairway just about every shot. I'd hit the green on my second or third shot. I'd sink the putt, I'd get my birdie, or I'd get a par, and frankly, it got a little boring."

So he remembered his long-range goal, which was to buy a ranch. His financial goal was to pay cash for it. Fortunately, he kept exact records for every round he shot in 1944. He knew exactly how he hit each drive, how he hit each chip, each putt, each iron shot. He knew exactly how he hit every single shot, and he noticed two things.

First of all, Byron noticed his lack of concentration, because the game had gotten boring for him. He also noticed that the shot he was missing the most was the chip-in. He never would have known those things if he had not kept those records.

So in 1945, he started making connections. He would say, "If I can chip this in, that will help me buy another cow. If I win this tournament, I can buy another ten acres of land." He identified each thing and tied them together.

The lesson we can get from both Byron and David Lofchick has to do with goals. David had goals of increasing his number of push-ups, sit-ups, and the distance he ran. He was willing to work very hard at that.

Remember, here's a guy who had no sense of balance. Every morning for one solid winter, he set his opportunity clock one hour earlier than any other member of the family. He'd wake up, he'd get his ice skates on, and he would crawl out to the frozen swimming pool, just to learn how to stand up.

How did David learn how to ride a bicycle? They hired a physical therapist. He would get on the bike, and the therapist would run behind him, stabilizing it until he could learn to maneuver without a sense of balance. He tore up a couple of bicycles before he was able to do it. He injured himself, scratching his knees primarily, a number of times.

Some kids are awfully cruel on occasion. Kids would run out at him, knowing he would have to swerve to miss them, and without a sense of balance, down he would go. Those were discouraging times. What would he do? He'd get right back up, and he'd go to it.

A lot of folks are not going to be nice to us as we go through life. A lot of times, they're going to get in our way. You have to want to succeed.

Never Give Up on Yourself

You might say, "Zig, let me tell you about that son or daughter of mine, or about some of the workers. They don't really have any desire. They're content to go through life in mediocrity. I do everything I can. I cannot get them inspired."

Why is desire so important? It is what changes the hot water of mediocrity to the steam of outstanding success. Little things do make big differences in life. It's the part of the blanket that hangs over the bed that keeps you warm. If you don't believe that, you've never been in the military and been short-sheeted.

If you're a sales manager, have you ever had a salesperson come to you and say, "Don't give me full commission on this one. I barely made it. Half commission would be OK"? You see, the difference between success and failure is frequently measured in just minute amounts.

A lot of people who say they don't want to are really saying, "I don't believe I can. The picture I have of myself is that of a loser." So we have to work on their confidence and self-esteem and convince them that they can, and desire will be born.

Find the Good News

Often people say, "I avoid the newspaper. It's full of bad news," but I read the newspaper every day, because you can find whatever you look for.

For ten years, I taught a large Sunday school class for forty-eight weeks out of the year, and I always started by reading the newspaper to the class. I would read them the good news they might have missed that week, because I can take any newspaper

> "Why is desire so important? It is what changes
> the hot water of mediocrity to the steam of
> outstanding success." —Zig Ziglar

in America and find something that is optimistic and upbeat and that I can use in my life. It depends on what you're looking for.

A lot of people, as I said earlier, find fault as if there was a reward for it. We need to start looking for some of the good things. Let me give you an example.

I read a column by Steve Blow in the *Dallas Morning News*, and he was talking about Tony Casillas, the big tackle for the Dallas Cowboys. He'd been over to Dallas's Sunset High School earlier, and he'd told the kids, "The eight of you who have the most attendance and the most improvement in your grades, I'm going take you out to dinner."

The competition was really tough. One of the winners was Israel Ramirez. Now Israel was making Ds and Fs on his grades. He got involved in this competition, and he ended up on the Honor Roll. As he put it, one thing that happened along the way was that he changed his friends. The friends he'd been running with were Ds and Fs and dropouts, so he changed his friends.

The *Los Angeles Times* did an extensive article, and it said that people who go to the top invariably, at one time in their lives, make conscious decision to associate with winners instead of losers. As the Bible says, "Be not deceived; evil companions corrupt good morals."

Having worked in the drug ward for a long time, I can tell you that if a youngster is running with kids who are doing drugs, the odds are eight times as great that he or she also is going to get involved in drugs. That's where peer pressure comes in.

In Deuteronomy 20:8, God says that if some guys don't want to fight, if they have a spirit of fear, send them home, because they will pollute and influence the others. They'll make them scared, and we'll end up losing the battle.

Associate with the right people is the message. One of the winners of Tony Casillas's dinners was a young man named Raymond Sanchez. Raymond had been taught right. His mom had brought him up on the right principles, but when he moved to the eighth grade, he went to a bigger school.

When kids change schools, they have to make new friends.

Many times, the kids who are involved in sexual activity, gangs, thievery, and this sort of thing look at them as fresh meat, and they zero in on them. And a lot of times a child moving into a new school wants to be accepted by just about anybody. There's your danger zone. That's when we really need to keep our eyes open.

When Raymond went to this new school, he noticed there was an eighth-grader there who ran the school. He was pretty cool, so Raymond started dressing like him, cutting his hair like him, walking like him, talking like him. This eighth-grader was in charge of drugs in the school. Soon Raymond was selling drugs. It started out as selling pot. It later moved to cocaine and Corvettes—literally.

Then the drive-by shootings started, and Raymond realized that things were not going well. When you look at influence, it works both ways. His girlfriend was going to Dallas Can Academy, which consists entirely of dropouts and kids that are in trouble. She said, "Raymond, this is a wonderful school. I'm learning some tremendous things." So he decided to get into that school. His girlfriend influenced him for the good.

After he'd been at the school for a couple of days, Raymond realized that his life was miserable. He had money, cars, girls and everything else, but he realized his life was miserable.

In the end Raymond graduated as the valedictorian of his class. The city of Dallas hired him for their gang intervention program, and today he's working with Dallas Can Academy. Grant East, who runs the academy, says he really is a unique young man.

I'm delivering another message here: never give up on our kids, although sometimes it's tempting. Never give up on yourself.

Values and Morals

As I've already emphasized, failure is an event; it is not a person. Yesterday ended last night. Today really is a new day.

When I was forty-five years old, I was stone broke and in debt. I'd worked and had a good attitude all of my life, but until I bought into these principles and change the picture I had of myself, my life was no different. The picture we have of ourselves is important, but I'm also saying that our values are important as well.

We're getting to the point where there are very few moral absolutes. One of my salespeople, Don Michaels, had an interesting phone conversation. A teacher called and was talking to him about some of the products we sell. The teacher said, "Well, now we cannot teach the kids what is right and what is wrong."

"Wait a minute," said Don. "You can't tell them what's right and wrong?"

"No, that's judgmental; we simply present the facts. We can't tell them what's right and what's wrong."

"I'm a little puzzled now," Don said. "You can't tell them what's wrong, but if they do wrong, we put them in jail. Now is that fair?"

Moral absolutes, I believe, are important. A lot of times people say, "You talk about values, but whose values?" Well, I have a list. I challenge parents, I challenge educators, I challenge anybody to go down the list, and tell me which one do you not want your child to be taught?

Do you not want them to be taught honesty? How about character? How about responsibility? Discipline, is that OK? How about commitment and enthusiasm and a positive mental attitude?

I am not talking religion; I'm talking about values. In our "I Can" course, we teach no religion, but we do teach values.

John F. Kennedy, I think, expressed it quite well. This is an excerpt from the speech he would have made in Dallas the day he was shot: "We, in this country, in this generation, are—by destiny rather than by choice—the watchmen on the walls of world freedom. We ask, therefore, that we may be worthy of our power and responsibility, that we may exercise our strength with wisdom and restraint, that we may achieve in our time and for all times the ancient vision of peace on earth, goodwill toward men. That must always be our goal, and the righteousness of our call must always underlie our strength, for as it was written long ago: 'Except the Lord keep the city, the watchman waketh but in vain.'"

I agree. That's how our country was built. We're a values-oriented society.

"We in this country, in this generation, are—by destiny rather than by choice—the watchmen on the walls of world freedom." —President John Kennedy

---

The Nonexistent Free Lunch

How many of you would prefer to have somebody who was honest and worked hard and was enthusiastic? Isn't that a silly question? Yet it's one that has to be answered.

One of my favorite stories along these lines was told many years ago. A king called all of his wise men together. He said, "I want you to compound for me the wisdom of the ages. I want you to put it in bound book form."

They went out, and they wrote a long time. They came back with twelve huge volumes. The king looked at them, and he said, "I'm sure this is the wisdom of the ages, but it's too lengthy. People won't read it; you have to condense it."

They came back with just one volume, and then a chapter, then a page, and finally a paragraph, but the king kept telling them to condense it. Ultimately they came back with one sentence. When he looked at it, they king said, "Hey, that's it. As soon as all men everywhere learn this, most of our problems will be solved." The sentence simply said, "There ain't no free lunch."

Folks, that's an important message. There really ain't no free lunch. We do have to work. The family of success has work as the father and integrity as the mother. Get along with the parents, and you won't have any trouble with the rest.

Work is the foundation of all business, the source of all prosperity, and the parent of genius. Work can do more to advance youth than their own parents, be they ever so wealthy. It is represented in the humblest savings and has laid the foundation of every fortune. It is the salt that gives life its savor, but it must be loved before it can bestow the greatest blessing and achieve its greatest end.

When loved, work makes life sweet, purposeful, and fruitful. I know I'm dealing in a lot of clichés. Some people are quick to condemn them, but what is a cliché? It is a truth that has retained its validity through time. Mankind would lose half its hard-earned wisdom, built up patiently over the ages, if it ever lost its clichés.

Another little one: there aren't any hard and fast rules for getting ahead in the world, just hard ones. Do you agree with that one? Is success easy? Is anything easy? No, but it can be fun, and that's the thing we keep trying to emphasize.

The most practical, beautiful philosophy in all the world won't work if you won't. Education covers a lot of ground, but it won't cultivate any of it.

One of my favorite stories has to do with something that happened many years ago. It seems that there was a hot day out in the Midwest. A crew was working on a section of the railroad when a luxury train appeared, with four cars, of which the last was a gorgeous caboose.

A window opened on the luxurious last car, and a voice called out. "Dave, is that you? Dave Anderson, over here." Dave Anderson was leading the work crew in the hot sun, and Jim Murphy was the voice calling. He said, "Come on over, Dave. I want to talk to you."

Dave was very happy to get out of the hot sun into that air-conditioned car, so he walked over, and he and Jim greeted each other warmly outside. They went in and had a marvelous visit for about an hour. Dave and Jim shook hands, then Dave went back to his work crew.

One of the workers said, "Dave, do you know who that is?"

"Why, sure. It's Jim Murphy, president of the railroad."

"How do you know Jim Murphy so well?"

"On the same day over twenty years ago, he and I went to work for this railroad."

"Dave, how do you explain that? You are still out here working in the sun, and he is in an air-conditioned car and president of the railroad."

Dave Anderson's answer is one of the great lessons of life. He said, "Over twenty years ago, I went to work for $1.75 an hour. Jim Murphy went to work for the railroad."

It's a two-way street. The company needs to provide training, inspiration, and opportunity. When the worker provides excitement, enthusiasm, commitment, and honest effort, both management and workers are on the same side. When that happens, productivity is no longer a problem.

Crazy for You

The redhead and I had an opportunity to see the musical *Crazy for You*. We were enthralled. I almost never see anything without thinking, how can I use this? What am I learning? That's where I get my biggest enjoyment. As I watched those twenty-seven or twenty-eight performers, I was fascinated, and I said, "We can learn some lessons from this."

To begin with, every singer and dancer was expending total effort. They gave it their all, and they were giving their all at the end just as they were at the beginning. Their enthusiasm was contagious. They had a conviction that their role made the difference in whether it was going to be a successful presentation or not. You know what? They were right.

It's the same old story: for want of the nail, the shoe was lost, for want of the shoe, the horse was lost, for want of the horse, the rider was lost, for want of the rider, the battle was lost, for want of the battle, the country was lost. Often one person breaks down, and particularly in small companies, that does create a lot of problems.

The guys and gals in that musical were committed to doing their absolute best. They were giving it their all. You could just feel and see the way they were encouraging each other. "Come on," as if to say, "You can do it, you can do it," and they were there pulling for one another. If one was singing, the others would be looking at him, and you could just feel their encouragement. (Think what that would do in the attitude of most companies.) Their team spirit was absolutely beautiful. They knew they were functioning as one, and there was a lot of trust involved.

I don't know if you've ever watched dancers, but you have to be in good physical shape. You have to be an athlete to do a lot of those things. At one point, the star of the show is cavorting all over the place, and for five minutes, he never even looks behind. Then he comes up, there's a big drop-off behind, and without even glancing behind, back he goes.

If somebody's not there to catch that actor, he is seriously injured. He had the trust because of all the things that had happened before. That brings up timing; the timing of what we do is important. They were having fun; they were having an enormously good time in doing what they were doing.

I believe that whatever the job is, somewhere along the way we can all can get some enjoyment out of it. There's a bit of humor in almost everything.

I know this is going to sound like cruel humor, but he laughed the loudest himself after he got through crying. Jim Norman, the CEO of our company, was walking in one day, and it was slippery out front. He slipped and ended up flat out on the ground. About half the people saw him there, and they thought that was the funniest thing ever. Obviously he was not hurt, or they would not have been laughing.

What's funny about seeing somebody fall? Have you ever fallen? Don't you feel the silliest you've ever felt in your life? (If it doesn't hurt, that is.) You're just so embarrassed.

It happened to me recently. We were riding in the tram out at DFW. You know how they always say, "Hold on to something," but shoot, I know everything is going to be all right. So I'm just standing there, you know, and all of a sudden, bam. They put the brakes on, and I went tumbling down like a ton of bricks. After I got over the shock and a little embarrassment (and fortunately, I was not hurt), I thought it was funny too. You can have some fun at it.

The guys and gals in that show were hard workers. They were giving it their all. Put that to work in your personal life, in the school, in the family, in the company, and you'll be amazed at the results.

Now let me tell you the rest of the story. Probably no more than 10 percent of the people who are reading this are not making more money than everybody in that production, except maybe the top three or four people. Theater is one of the most uncertain industries in all the world.

Why do the performers do it? In the first place, they love to do it, number one. In the second place, every one of them has a conviction deep down that they someday are going to make it big. The odds are astronomical that they won't, but without that hope, there is not going to be any chance at all.

Whatever you do, the odds are considerably higher that the same effort, the same enthusiasm, the same commitment to rehearsing over and over will determine how far you go on the job. You prepare before you go to work.

Another major point: when it was all over, had there been no applause for all that effort, that play would long ago have died. Shakespeare said that the

applause of a single human being is of great conse-
quence. All of us need applause.

My friend James Howard is a consultant who does
motion studies and productivity studies for our company. He says that in answer to the question, what
does management say when you complete a task?
Ninety-four percent of employees replied that management says nothing. Think of what a downer that
is. Apply the principle of applause, and we can get so
much more done in our lives.

The Loser's Limp

Why don't people develop their talents and work as
hard as they're capable of doing? Denial is the first
thing. Denying that you have the ability and the talent gives you the loser's limp, that excuse: "You can't
expect much from me, because I haven't gotten much."
That's why so much of this book has been dedicated to
changing the picture you have of yourself.

One of my favorite stories takes place at the turn
of the last century down in Beaumont, Texas. A man
was selling his property bit by bit because there was
a depression on and a drought. An oil company executive came along, and said, "Sir, we think there's oil
underneath your property. Let us drill for oil. If we
discover it, we will pay you royalties on every barrel."

The man had nothing to lose and a great deal to
gain, so he said, "Let's do it."

They drilled for the oil. In those days, the derricks were made out of wood. When they brought in a gusher, the force of the gusher destroyed the derrick. The greater the destruction, the greater the excitement.

When this one came in, it blew the derrick to smithereens, and for the next eleven days, hundreds of thousands of barrels of oil poured out before they could put the cap on it. It was Spindletop, the single most productive oil well in history. Three major oil companies were born out of that field that day. The man became an instant millionaire. Or did he?

In reality, he'd been a millionaire many times over ever since he had acquired the property, but until they discovered the oil, brought it to the surface, took it to the marketplace, and cashed it in, it had no value.

It doesn't make a difference how much ability you have unless you recognize that ability, confess it (you thought confession was a dirty word, didn't you?), and develop it, it really does not have value.

A lot of people never get started. They're procrastinators. Tomorrow is the greatest labor-saving device ever invented. A lot of people never do things. They're going to, but not today.

It doesn't make a difference how much ability you have unless you recognize that ability, confess it, and develop it, it really does not have value.

Then there's the fear of failure that I talked about in the goal setting segment we dealt with. What is fear? As I've already pointed out, it forms an acrostic for *False Evidence Appearing Real.*

Another reason a lot of people don't advance is that they are self-centered and irresponsible. "That's not my deal. Here's what I want to do. I want to do my thing." They never accept responsibility for using their own abilities. They're deeply involved in the blame game. Blame somebody else. Blame society. Blame everybody.

Furthermore, a lot of them say, "I deserve better than that. I want to start at the top." Isn't that something? The only people who really start at the top are gravediggers, and as you know, they end up in the hole.

As I've already pointed out, immigrants have four times as good a chance of becoming a millionaire as do native-born Americans. That's because when they come in America, they're gung-ho about taking a minimum wage job, because minimum wage for them is maximum wage where they came from. They don't look for a better opportunity. They look for the opportunity and make it better. There's a difference right there. That is a very important point.

Chapter 7

Hamburger Flipping

One night at around 11:00, the chairman of the board comes walking into one of his company's fast-food restaurants. No customers are in there. He looks around but doesn't see anybody at the counter. Then in the back he sees a guy smoking a cigarette. He just about hits the ceiling.

The chairman goes charging around. Not only is the clerk who's supposed to be up front smoking a cigarette, but the manager is sitting back there, also smoking. The chairman reads them a riot act. He tears that guy apart all up and down, but the manager is pretty cool about it.

Finally, when the chairman has finished reaming him out, the manager says, "And just who are you?"

"I'm the chairman of the board of this company. Now what do you think about that?"

The guy is very cool. He says, "I think you and I both are about as high in this organization as we're ever going to go."

I tell this story for this reason. I get irritated when on the news, I hear celebrities and athletes say, "You'll end up flipping hamburgers in a fast-food restaurant." I want to talk about the hamburger flippers of life, because I happen to believe that any work that is honest, that is productive, that does a service, is a good job.

Of course I use the term "hamburger flippers" loosely. Obviously a lot of fast-food places have pizza, chicken and 1,001 other things, but they always use the term "hamburger flippers" when they're putting them down. Let me talk about jobs like this.

First of all, a fast-food job teaches youngsters discipline and responsibility. Second, it teaches them pride in performance. Many of them learn for the first time the importance of personal grooming, being neatly dressed, and being dependable. They learn the value of money and thrift when they start buying things themselves and discover that their money will not buy everything in sight.

They did a study out in California with high-school students who were getting ready to drop out. They would ask them, "Now what are you going to do?"

The students would say, "I'm going to get a job, I'm going to rent a little apartment, and then I'm going to get a car." They start enumerating those things, but they could not even get close to earning as much money as is required for that. Think of the advantage they would have had, had they been working ten or twelve hours and learned exactly how much they could buy with that money.

I'm grateful that, as a youngster, I was able to work in a grocery store in Yazoo City. I was a teller in that store. I'm not trying to impress you with the title; it just meant I told people to move while I swept. I mean, it wasn't in management.

In the summer months, our business was awfully slow. I vividly remember the day that the boss was trying to get all of us busy, although there was nothing to do.

I said, "Mr. Anderson, what do you want me to do?"

"You can dust these shelves. You can clean them out. You can rearrange them." He pointed to a shelf that had two cans of tomatoes in it.

"Mr. Anderson, there are just two cans of tomatoes."

I guess the way I said "just two cans" got to him. He grabbed me by the shoulders and said, "Let me tell you something about those two cans of tomatoes, boy. First of all, it started out with a case, and that's twenty-four cans. We sold twenty-two. That means we have all of our money back. The two cans there represent profit, and profit is what enables us to stay open, and that's the way you get your salary. Now what do you think of those two cans of tomatoes?"

"Mr. Anderson," I said, "those are the two most beautiful cans of tomatoes I have ever seen in my life. They're absolutely gorgeous." I learned a very important lesson about what economics and profit really meant. They meant my job.

In fast-food places you learn a great deal about courtesy and human relations. You learn a lot about teamwork, working together, and the importance of being committed. When you say you're going to be there, the rest of the team is counting on you to be there.

You also might be surprised at how much some of these young people make. I've seen twenty-two- and twenty-three-year-olds managing places that do a million dollars' worth of business a year. You know what? They're making $50,000 and $60,000 a year. Several of those establishments give the managers an automobile.

You take a sixteen-year-old and put him in a place like that—and the manager is just seven or eight years older, with that kind of success. Fast-food work is effective. Young people learn goal setting, and they depend on themselves to do things. That is so important.

I wonder how many young people these jobs will keep out of drugs and crime. Surely the people who are ridiculing them don't think it would be better for them to get into something of that nature.

Another thing: a lot of businesspeople go into fast-food restaurants. How many times has a clerk been given a better or bigger opportunity because they were especially nice to a customer?

As I mentioned earlier, immigrants are four times as likely to become millionaires in America as are the native-born, because immigrants take a job and make an opportunity out of it. Too many of the native-born take an opportunity and make a job out of it. Attitude does make a difference.

There are a lot of part-time jobs. You can start in lawn care. I remember when we first moved to Dallas. Our yard man was Black. His name was David Smith. David initially only finished the seventh grade. Years later, he went back to school and graduated from high school at age twenty-four.

David started out just cutting yards. Then he started studying how to care for lawns and how to do all of the things that go with landscaping. He put his three daughters through university. Two of them ended up as teachers, because he started where he could start and took it from there.

The same thing frequently happens in janitorial jobs for corporate maintenance. Several years ago, a lady from Chicago came through our "Born to Win" program. She was a beauty queen. The only job she could get starting out was in janitorial maintenance.

"Immigrants are four times as likely to become millionaires in America as are the native-born, because immigrants take a job and make an opportunity out of it. Too many of the native-born take an opportunity and make a job out of it." —Zig Ziglar

She ended up three years later with her own company and over a hundred employees working for her. It's not where you start that's important; it's where you go.

A youngster might start out as a babysitter and decide to have a professional babysitting service. Housecleaning can develop into exactly the same thing.

In our society today, many people are having to start over. As I have stressed, job security is pretty much a thing of the past, but employment security is the greatest it's ever been for certain people who believe certain things and take certain steps, which I've been talking about throughout this book. But when disaster strikes—and it does strike frequently—how do you handle it?

Several years ago, a good friend of mine in Atlanta was worth several million dollars one day, and a few days later he wasn't worth anything. It had all been wiped out. We were talking about it, and I said, "How do you feel?"

"Well," he said, "Zig, I'm not exactly on cloud 87, jumping up and down with excitement: 'Oh boy, I've lost all of my money.' I can start all over, but I will tell you this. I made a very foolish mistake that led to the loss of my money. I know a lot more now than I did when I first got started. The principles I've used to get there will take me right back again. It's no big deal. I'm simply going to do the same thing again." And he did.

Chapter 8

Lessons from Dave Longaberger

What does it take to be successful? Let me share this with you. It's a story that I believe represents the American dream. I'm going to talk about one individual and his company a little bit, mainly because I believe it will give every reader a considerable amount of hope, and hope is the most important ingredient I have to sell. Again, if there's hope in the future, there is power in the present.

This particular individual is named Dave Longaberger. It took him two years to get out of the first grade; it took him three years to get out of the fifth. He was twenty years old when he finished high school. He was functioning at the eighth-grade level, and incidentally he had epilepsy and he stuttered.

Look at that profile and tell me what his chances are in life. Last year, though, his company did in excess of $200 million worth of business, and they project over a billion-dollar yearly business in several years. How did he get there? What happened along the way?

Let's do a little exploring. When he was seven years old, he went to work in a grocery store; there he learned something that can be helpful to each one of us in our careers. He learned that the best way to keep the boss off of his back was to anticipate what the boss wanted and do it before the boss had to tell him. How many of you employers like that kind of an employee? Doesn't that give him employment security right there?

What did Dave do as a child? He started shoveling snow, mowing grass, delivering papers, and hauling trash. His family started calling him the 25-cent millionaire. Isn't it ironic sometimes how when you hang a label on somebody like that, it does take place?

Dave was a student of life. See, most times we miss some of the most obvious things. For example, if you are wearing a wristwatch right now, do not look at it.

Have you had your wristwatch for at least a year? Did you know the average American looks at their wristwatch over two hundred times a day? (Of course that includes the last few minutes before lunch and the last few minutes before the end of the day.) That's a lot of times. If you've had your watch a year, that means you've looked at it thousands of times. You ought to know what's there, shouldn't you?

I'm going to ask you three questions about your watch. I'll bet you can't get them all right.

1. Does your wristwatch have regular numerals or Roman numerals?
2. Does it have numbers at all, or are they slashes or dots or blanks or emblems or none of the above?
3. What is at the 12:00 slot? What's at the 3:00 slot? What's at the 6:00 slot? What's at the 9:00 slot?

Now that you've thought about it, I want you, maybe for the first time since you've owned your watch, to look at it very carefully.

Now that you have, I want to ask you another question: what time is it? The truth of the matter is, most of us miss a lot of the things that go on in life.

Dave Longaberger was not a brilliant student in school, but he was a brilliant student in life. Early on, he started learning by observing things. For example, they had fourteen children in the family, but they only had one bathroom. One of his early goals was to have his own bathroom, and if you don't think one minute is important, it depends entirely on which side of the bathroom door you're on.

Dave learned to set goals early on. He discovered that if he worked in a certain way and did certain things, he had a better chance to get the things that he wanted. When he opened his restaurant, when he sold Fuller brushes, when he did anything, he always thought in terms of *my* customers—not the company's customers, but *my* customers. He knew if he treated his customers properly, he had a chance to improve himself and his business.

One thing Dave learned was this: all jobs involve people skills. It doesn't make a difference what the job is; it is a person-to-person thing. He also learned that any job could be fun. He discovered that the more he enjoyed his work and showed it, the more fun the customers had and the more they bought from him.

Dave learned from everybody and everywhere he went. He was in the Army for a spell, and he learned the advantages of uniformity, control, and consistency, and of having a central headquarters. He went to graduate school in life.

Dave was a risk taker. There's risk in everything we do. He scraped up a few dollars to open a little restaurant in Dresden, Ohio. He had already had a little grocery store. When he got ready to open his restaurant, he had $135 in cash left.

He bought $135 worth of food to serve breakfast with. When he had sold breakfast, he went back to the store and bought the food for lunch. When he finished lunch, he bought some more food for dinner, and that's the way it got started.

His family had been in the basket-making business years earlier. His dad had quit making them, except for a few along the way. In 1965, Dave decided to reopen the business. Every member of his family said, "Dave, you can't do that." They tried to discourage him, but he'd been looking at imported baskets, and they weren't of the same quality that they'd been making, so he decided to get back in the business.

Was it always spectacularly successful? No way. In 1986, they owed over $5.5 million. There were about five thousand people involved, most of them in making and distributing baskets.

With all of that debt, Dave went to his employees and said, "You know, I've always been upfront and straightforward and told you the truth. This business is going to make it. I'm going to ask you to trust me, and in some way or other, we will pay the bill." Because his word had always been his bond, everybody stayed with him.

What does he do that is different? He makes every person feel important. Every basket that is produced by his company carries the signature of the person who made it. Dave Longaberger makes every individual know that they are unique.

He has a unique management style too. He doesn't have the supervisors evaluating the workers; he has the workers evaluating the supervisors. When those evaluations come in, he knows what he has to do.

Dave Longaberger is a people person almost to an extreme. He says that if you take care of your people, they're going to take care of you. If you let them shine and make them important, they'll want to come to work. Then it becomes not just a job, but a family of people.

Dave's perspective is always solid. He uses common sense in virtually everything. He operates on the principle of the Golden Rule, and he says competition is the best thing that ever happened to him, because your competition will point out your weaknesses. They're the best source of information. They will teach you things.

The really big thing that happened to him was that he learned to appreciate his own uniqueness; he realized he was different. He knew he loved people; he respected people; he got along with people. He started using the things that he did have. He also believed that every company should put something back into the community in which it is operating.

As a result, Dresden, Ohio, is one of the neatest, cleanest cities that you will ever find. It's a small place, but Dave's company pays for cutting the grass up and down Main Street, because it attracts visitors. Of course the fact that they have this nice factory there and these restaurants there gives him a reason for doing that, but he is the one who initiated that action.

He truly has an over-the-top attitude. He moved his company from survival to stability from the time they'd gotten so deeply in debt, from stability to success, and from success to significance. I believe that's what life really has to offer.

Chapter 9

The Water Pump

Now I want to talk about a water pump—an old-fashioned water pump. If you will get the message of the pump, this alone will do you a tremendous amount of good in your personal, family, and business life.

I have a couple of good friends down in south Alabama: Bernard Haygood and Jimmy Glenn. One day they were out riding through the foothills in their area. Bernard was driving. It was a hot August day, and as they were riding along, they got awfully thirsty. They saw an old, abandoned farmhouse, and Bernard drove in behind it. He looked over, and sure enough, there was an old pump. He hopped out of the car, ran over, grabbed the handle, and started to pump.

He'd been pumping a few minutes, and he said, "Jimmy, you'd better get that old bucket over there and dip some water out of the creek. We're going to have to prime this pump a little bit."

Do you know what I'm talking about when I talk about priming the pump? Priming the pump simply means that you have to put something up there before you can expect to get anything out of the pump itself. That's really one of the stories of life, isn't it?

Many people stand in front of the stove of life and say, "Now, stove, you give me something to eat. Then I'll put the wood in you." Many times the employee goes to the employer and says, "Give me a raise, and then I'll start coming to work on time. Give me a raise, and then I'll start doing what you've been paying me to do." Many times the student goes to the teacher and says, "Teacher, if I flunk this course, my mama is going to skin me alive. Give me a passing grade this quarter, and I'll guarantee you that next go-around I will really study." They're really saying, "Reward me, and then I'll perform," but that is not the way life works.

Imagine a farmer saying, "Lord, it's true I didn't plant a thing this year, but if you'll give me a big crop, next year I'll plant more than anybody in this whole county. I absolutely guarantee it."

That is not the way you work. You put something in before you can honestly expect to get something out.

Back to our story. It's August, it's hot, and old Bernard is working up a real sweat pumping away.

Priming the pump simply means you have to put something up there before you can expect to get anything out of the pump itself. It's one of the stories of life. You put something in before you can honestly expect to get anything out.

Finally he says, "You know, Jimmy, I just don't believe there's any water down there."

Jimmy says, "Bernard, this is south Alabama, and in south Alabama the wells are deep, and we're glad they are, because the deeper the well, the cooler, the cleaner, the sweeter, the purer, the better-tasting the water."

Bernard was just working, and he was sweating more and more. How much pumping are you going to do for a drink of water? Finally, he threw up his hands and said, "Jimmy, there just ain't any water down there."

"Don't stop, Bernard, don't stop," said Jimmy. "If you do, the water goes all the way back down, and you're going to have to start all over."

We'll never know how much good work is lost because somebody didn't do just a little bit more. As students, how many times were we given a difficult problem, and we'd work on it with no results? We'd go to the teacher and say, "Teacher, there's no solution to this problem. You've given us a phony here to test us."

The teacher would just smile and say, "Give it another shot." You gave it another shot, and all of a sudden what had been such a mystery before becomes crystal-clear. A lot of times, just a little more effort is really all we need. If we pump long enough and hard enough and enthusiastically enough, eventually the effort is going to be followed with a reward, and the water will start to flow. Once the water starts to flow, all you need is a little good, steady effort, and you'll be getting rewards that are absolutely unbelievable.

Have you ever noticed this? When things are bad, they get worse; when they're good, they get much better. It has nothing whatever to do with what's going on out there. It has everything to do with what's going on right here.

I love the story of the pump because it's a story of life. It has nothing to do with your age or education, with whether you're black or white, whether you're male or female, old or young, an introvert or an extrovert, educated or uneducated. It has everything to do with your God-given right as free people to work as long as you wish, as hard as you wish, and as enthusiastically as you wish to get the things out of life that you really want.

When they tackle a new project, an awful lot of people will say, "I'll just give it a little try. If it works out, that will be good, and if it doesn't work out, that's OK too. Nothing ventured, nothing gained."

But when you get into something, you need to really get after it until you get the water to flow. Steady effort is what's going to make the big difference.

One of the most debilitating things that can ever happen to a talented, educated, capable person is to get a job as a hamburger flipper. These people get a job that is "beneath" them, give it a half-hearted effort, and get fired because they're not productive. "What do you mean firing me?" they say. "I have all this education. I can do all of these things. Why would you fire me?" Very simple: you are not productive.

The story of the pump is the story of life. Now this requires a tremendous amount of discipline. We've been talking about that throughout. It requires character, it requires persistence.

A Will to Live

On March 10, 1981, on a beautiful clear day, a young man was flying his airplane. His name was Morris Goodman, and he was an enormously successful life insurance salesman. He had been taking care of himself all of his life, had succeeded in everything that he had attempted to do. However, that particular day, something went awry with the plane, and he ended up in a very serious crash. His spinal cord was crushed. Half the muscles and ligaments in his neck were destroyed. His neck was broken at the first and second vertebrae. His jaw was crushed, as were his larynx and voice box. The nerves in his diaphragm were so badly damaged that it wouldn't work, and he couldn't breathe on his own. He was unable to swallow. His bowels, bladder, and kidneys stopped functioning.

All the experts said that the odds of survival were over a million to one, and if he did survive, he would simply be a vegetable. The situation was not good, but Morris Goodman said something that I think is enormously significant. He said, "The doctors were basing their opinions on test results and past cases. I was basing my expectations to fully recover on a will to live and a will to recover."

This is the classic concept of optimism and positive thinking, along with a deep belief in the potential within each one of us. Morris had succeeded in everything he had tried. He'd been taking care of his body by doing the proper things, eating the right food from a nutritional point of view, exercising, and following a strict regimen all of his life.

He was in a position now where the odds were so enormously high that he would apparently never be able to do anything. He couldn't communicate with anybody, so his sister devised a card system that enabled him to blink his eyes and communicate effectively with people. He went through a lot of turmoil, a lot of difficulty along the way.

On November 13, 1981, just a few months after they said he would not live, Morris walked out of that hospital. Today he's been bear hunting and deer hunting. He travels all over the world speaking. He's running a camp for underprivileged boys, giving them a chance in life.

They made a movie about him, *The Miracle Man*, and I'm delighted to be able to say that the movie says quite a bit about the fact that he was listening to my motivational tapes. He said it made a difference. It helped his attitude when things were tough.

You look at the picture of this guy, and here's what you find. Number one, from the first day he visualized himself as walking out of there, healthy and hunting. He had the capacity to focus, to zero in on that one goal. He had a tremendous desire and will to win. He had the discipline and the commitment, and he had the persistence that was going to be necessary.

President Calvin Coolidge had this to say: "Nothing in the world can take the place of persistence. Talent will not; nothing is more common that unsuccessful men with talent. Genius will not; unrewarded genius is almost a proverb. Education will not; the world is full of educated derelicts. Persistence, determination, and hard work makes the difference."

I've talked a lot about total success in the game of life. I sometimes fear that because I've said so little about money, a lot of people may think that I don't

---

"Nothing in this world can take the place of persistence. Talent will not; nothing is more common than unsuccessful men with talent. Genius will not; unrewarded genius is almost a proverb. Education will not; the world is full of educated derelicts. Persistence, determination and hard work makes the difference."
—President Calvin Coolidge

---

have an interest in financial success. Absolutely I do. As I said earlier, anybody that says they're not interested in money will lie about other things too. I believe that's absolutely true, but money is just one of the things in life.

I want to tell you something, because a lot of people are unaware of this: millionaires are boring. As I said earlier, less than 1 percent of all of the millionaires in America are involved in athletics, music, television, and the movies all combined, but 99 percent plus of them are people just like you and me.

A Louis Harris poll of people who earned over $142,000 a year and had a net worth of over a half million dollars, not including their homes, described these successful people as unexciting, middle-aged, and cautious. They emphasized family values and the work ethic; 83 percent of them were married; 96 percent of them acquired their net worth through hard work; 80 percent were politically conservative or middle of the road; and they were relatively non-materialistic. In other words, their goals went beyond money: 85 percent said that their major objective was to provide for their family. Only 11 percent rated owing an expensive car as being high on their totem pole. Prestige and the badge of success don't matter to them nearly as much as family, education, and their business or job.

These people don't have much excitement, but they have lots of happiness. They have a good standard of living, but infinitely more importantly, they have an excellent quality of life. Persistence, consistency, discipline, and hard work make the difference. Their lives seem to be in balance.

Another study by Thomas J. Stanley in *Medical Economics*, July 20, 1992, showed almost exactly the same thing. The profile of a wealthy person is this: hard work, perseverance, and most of all self-discipline. The average wealthy person has lived all his adult life in the same town. He's been married once and is still married. He lives in a middle-class neighborhood next to people with a fraction of his wealth. He's a compulsive saver and investor. He's made his money on his own: 80 percent of America's millionaires are first-generation rich. Sounds like opportunity is still alive and well in our great country.

Attitude is the greatest difference between millionaires and the rest of us. They skimp on luxuries, but are more willing to pay top dollar for good legal and financial advice. The self-made rich develop clear goals for their money.

Once I got an extremely exciting bit of correspondence. A young man named Rick Roussin, who lives in Northridge, California, said, "Seven years ago, I was strung out on drugs and alcohol. I was completely bankrupt in all areas of my life: financially, physically, spiritually, and emotionally."

Rick Roussin said that he was a high-school dropout, with no formal education or business experience, but he did have a burning desire and a willingness to change. "I knew for things to change, *I* had to change. For things to get better, *I* had to get better." I love that.

"In order to change," he said, "I started going to AA. There's where you find help." You see, the Twelve-Step programs will not work unless the person who is being treated does something for somebody else. The only way they can stay sober is by sharing the benefits of sobriety to others. They're on call.

A couple of members of my family were participants in AA. They would get calls at midnight and 3:00 in the morning, and they would get up and go to be with that person to help them get the through the crisis. They will tell you a thousand times that that's the only way that they were able to beat their alcohol problem.

That was Rick's first step to a better life. He said, "I developed some faith in the future and shut the door on the past." Boy, that is so important. You have to make friends with the past in order to focus on the present so you can make your tomorrow what it is capable of being.

The first two years Rick got on this program, he drove an old 1967 Dodge Dart, rented a house, and then sublet several of the rooms just to make the rent each month. He said he was patient. It was tough getting started, but as he continued to go to the meetings, and he started learning about the health aspects of success, he went from weighing over 200 pounds down to 163 pounds. He's now thirty-two years old, and he says he's in the best shape of his life.

Rick said, "I started reading affirmations," whereby you claim the qualities of success. "I've been reading affirmations in the morning and before bed for over six years, and it's made a dramatic difference in my life. I always am telling people I'm feeling supergood, but I'm getting better. I always like to emphasize that they might not get anything out of it, but it makes me feel good in the very process of saying this."

"My belief system completely changed," Rick added. He went from thinking he was not worth $500 a week to believing he was worth over $25,000 a week. He bought the idea that you can have what you want if you help enough other people get what they want.

Last year he earned in excess of $300,000. He lives in a home worth over $750,000. He wears nice clothes, all of the things that everybody says they want, but he summed it up by saying, "The important thing is I have a wife and two beautiful children, and I have more delight in my family than any other phase of my life. My family life is infinitely better than it was. I wake up, and I look forward to what I'm going to do that day. I love my life. I love the people around me."

Rick goes ahead to say he came from what had been a dysfunctional family for generation after gen-

eration: divorce, alcoholism, child abuse, and everything else. He changed his direction in every area of
life physically, mentally, spiritually. He has changed,
and changed completely.

Why do I say that? If you don't like who you are
and where you are, don't sweat it. You're not stuck
there. You absolutely can grow. You absolutely can
change.

Chapter 10
One Last Look at Success

Let's take one last look at success. From my perspective, if I had the opportunity to make millions and millions of dollars but in the process destroyed my health and sacrificed my integrity, I would have said, "No deal." I'd be unwilling to give those things up in order to have the dollars, and I'm confident that you feel exactly the same way.

Yet many people still identify success with money. They talk about the biggest crook in town—the guy that lives in the biggest house, drives the biggest cars, takes the most trips.

Every time you see one of those people, ask yourself these questions: I wonder how happy he is. I wonder how healthy he is. I wonder how secure he is. I wonder how many friends he has. I wonder how much peace of mind he has. I wonder what his family relationships are. I wonder what his hope for a future really is.

If you think about it, you are going to be dead longer than you're going to be alive. The Bible says, "Seek ye first the Kingdom of God, and all these things shall be added unto you. For what profit is it to a man to gain the whole world and lose his own soul?"

The philosophy we're talking about will enable you to go all the way to the top, but let me tell you what that means. Suppose one of my children came to me and said, "Dad, it would have meant everything to me if, when I was a child, I could ever have known you as my dad. Had you ever been there in the morning to give me a pep talk when I was going off to school to face a tough test or a bully or trouble with my boyfriend, Dad, it would have meant so much. Had you been there at night to hug away some of my hurts, kiss away some of my tears, and give me some of the advice that you've given people all over the world—had that happened, Dad, maybe my life would not have turned out to be the disaster it has."

Had that happened to me, I would be one more brokenhearted dad, because like most parents, I deeply love my children. I'm so grateful I was able to dedicate my book *Raising Positive Kids in a Negative World*, to my four as being the most positive—and, I could have added, the most morally sound and sane—kids I know anywhere.

When you analyze it, you'll discover that every great failure in life is a moral failure. Ask Pete Rose. Ask Ivan Boesky, Michael Milken. Ask Jimmy Bakker and Jimmy Swaggert. Ask Jim Wright and Gary Hart.

Ask the legislators in South Carolina and Arizona, where by the score they turned crooked and were indicted for fraud. In recent decades in the State of Texas alone, three of our speakers of the House have been indicted—men that had brilliant futures and careers in front of them, but who became well-known failures.

Recently I was reading that in the State of Kentucky, for example, seven legislators, including the speaker of the House, were convicted on charges of bribery, extortion, obstruction of justice, mail fraud, racketeering, and so forth. As a matter of fact, at this moment, there are over 1,400 public officials under federal indictments. It caused one lady in the U.S. House to quip, "Don't tell my mother I'm a politician. She thinks I'm a prostitute."

When things get to that degree, we have reason to be concerned. It made somebody ask whether, when they call the roll in the House, you should answer "present" or "not guilty." There is growing concern among Americans about that political situation.

Yet in Kentucky they recognized something and passed a resolution. I'm just going to quote part of it, but it suggests that people may be now saying, "We have to look at our ethics, our values. We have to see what is going on."

This resolution, which the Kentucky House unanimously passed on the final day of a special session, is presented below. I'm only quoting a portion of it.

A resolution adjourning the 1993 extraordinary session on ethics in remembrance and honor of Jesus Christ, the Prince of Ethics.

Whereas on September 17, 1796, President George Washington stated, "Where is the security for property, for reputation, for life if the sense of religious obligation desert and let us, with caution, indulge the supposition that morality can be maintained without religion."

The resolution quotes Presidents John Adams and Thomas Jefferson. (I did not know Jefferson had written a book, *The Life and Morals of Jesus of Nazareth*. They passed out six thousand copies to people in the House and three thousand copies to people in the Senate.) It goes on to quote Benjamin Franklin, who said, "As to Jesus of Nazareth, I think his system of morals, as he left them to us, is the best the whole world ever saw or is likely to see."

I get excited when people start recognizing that there must be a turn in that direction. If, in my drive for fame and fortune, I'd broken the relationship with that beautiful redhead who's been my wife for nearly forty-seven years, I'd be the most brokenhearted man you've ever seen, because after over forty-six years, not only do I deeply love my wife, not only is

"As to Jesus of Nazareth, I think his system of morals, as he left them to us, is the best the whole world ever saw or is likely to see." —Benjamin Franklin

she by far the most important person on this earth to me, but I've just flat out got a crush on that redhead.

Somebody asked me one time, "What do you do for excitement?" I said, "I married it." I believe that's where the excitement is coming from. Some of you young whippersnappers who've only been married twenty-five or thirty years might not be able to relate to this, but after nearly forty-seven years, I find my wife to be more beautiful than she was on our wedding day. I'm so grateful that in doing all the things that I've been able to do that she's been at my side for them all.

As I've said, when I was forty-five years old, I was stone broke and in debt. We'd been married over twenty-seven years before I was ever able to give her something approaching financial security. Yet in all of those years, not once do I ever remember her saying, even one time, "Honey, if we just had more money, if we had more financial security, it would be so much better." She would always say, "Tomorrow is going to be better. You can do it." Then she would say those two things that mean so much to every man and every woman alive. "I love you, and I believe in you."

I cannot begin to tell you what it meant to me to have a cheerleader cheering me on every day of my life and praying for me every night of my life even as she, at this very moment, is praying for me.

Having a person who gives that kind of backing does make a difference. You see, a giant Belgian horse can pull 8,000 pounds on his own. Hook him up with another giant Belgian horse, and the team will pull 18,000 pounds. Send them off to school, teach them to pull in harmony, and the team will pull over 25,000 pounds.

Review the qualities of success as I've set them out here. Start claiming those qualities over and over with more excitement and enthusiasm, because the more you claim those qualities, the more you will have them. The more you have them in yourself, the more you'll be able to see them in your spouse, your employees, your brothers, your sisters, the people you live with. When you see them in yourself, it's easier to see them in others, and you treat people exactly as you see them. As you claim these qualities, you will deal more effectively with every person you're in contact with, and that's what's going to make the difference.

Whose Boy Are You?

I want to simply say this. Had I been on trial for my life, had you been my judge and jury and required me to tell me what I honestly believe you need to know in order for me to reap the most out of every phase of life, I would tell you another story.

When little Ben Hooper was born all those years ago in the foothills of east Tennessee, boys and girls like Ben, who had no idea who their daddies were, were ostracized. They were treated horribly. By the time the little guy was three years old, the other children would scarcely play with him. Parents were saying insane things like, "What's a boy like that doing playing with our children?" as if the child had anything to do with his own birth.

When Ben was six years old, they put him in the first grade. (They did not have kindergarten in those years.) They gave him a little desk as they did all the children, and at recess he would stay there, because none of the children would play with him.

Saturday was his toughest day of all. His mom would take him down to the little general store to buy supplies for the week. There were always other children there and other parents, and invariably one of them would make a caustic comment: "What's a boy like that doing around here?" Or, "Did you ever figure out who his daddy is?"

When Ben was twelve years old, a new preacher came to their little church in the foothills of east Tennessee. Almost immediately, Ben started hearing people talking about him, about how friendly and warm he was, how nonjudgmental he was, how he accepted each person as they were, how when he would walk into the room, the attitude, the atmosphere, the spirits would pick up. The preacher had the charisma that makes the difference. Ben liked to be around people like that.

One Sunday, though he had never been to church a day in his life, Ben Hooper decided to go. He got there late and left early. He did not want to attract any attention, but he liked what he heard. He was back there the next Sunday and the next, and the next.

To avoid attracting attention, he always got there late and left early. The message was so moving, so encouraging, so powerful and inspiring, it was almost as if there were a sign behind the minister's face that said, "For you, little Ben Hooper of unknown parentage. There is hope for you." I'll remind you again: if there's hope in the future, there is power in the present.

One Sunday Ben got so wrapped up in the message that he did not even realize that a number of people had come in and sat down behind him. He forgot all about the time, and suddenly the church services were over. He stood up, as did everyone else. He started to try to run out, but his passageway was blocked. He was trying to work his way through the crowd when he felt a hand on his shoulder.

He turned and look around, he looked up, and he was looking right into the eyes of the young minister, who asked him a question which had been on the minds of every person there for the previous twelve years. "Whose boy are you?"

Instantly the church grew deathly quiet. Then slowly a smile started to spread across the face of the young minister. It broke into a huge grin as he said, "Oh, I know whose boy you are. Why, the family resemblance is unmistakable. You are a child of God."

With that, the young minister swatted him across the rear and said, "That's quite an inheritance you have there, boy. Now go and see to it that you live up to it."

Many years later, Ben Hooper said that was the day he was elected governor of the State of Tennessee and later reelected. You see, the picture had changed. He'd gone from being a child of unknown heritage to a child of the King.

On July 4, 1972, though I had lost my earthly father when I was five years old, I took God up on his offer and became a child of the Heavenly King. I confessed Christ as Lord. That's when everything in my life changed. That changes hearts, and when you change hearts, that changes life.

Whose boy are you? Whose girl are you? Oh, I know whose child you are. Why, the family resemblance is unmistakable. You are a child of the King. That's quite an inheritance you have there.

The story is told of a father who was being harassed by his little boy when dad had some things to do. So he took a picture of a map of the world and cut it into a lot of pieces. He told his son to put it all back together, thinking he was going to have several minutes, maybe an hour, to catch up on his work.

In a matter of minutes, the little guy came back, and he had the picture all complete. His dad said, "Son, how on earth did you do that?"

The little guy said, "Dad, I just turned the picture over, and on the other side of the map of the world, there was a picture of a man. When I got the man together, the world was together."

That's what this book is all about: get your life together, and then your world will come together. You have to *be* before you can *do*, and you have to *do* before you can *have*. I've placed in your hands a set of tools that will enable you to be what you need to be in order to do what you need to do in order to have what you want to have.

Buy the ideas, use these tools every day, follow these instructions, because if you do, I'll see you, and yes, I really do mean you, at the top.

You have to *be* before you can *do*, and
you have to *do* before you can *have*.

Appendix

The Ziglar
Goal Setting System

The Chinese say that the journey of a thousand leagues begins with a single step. Commit yourself to take these goal-setting steps NOW.

BAD NEWS: To properly set your goals you will need to invest a minimum of ten hours and possibly as many as twenty hours. That's one of the reasons only 3% of the population have clearly defined their objectives in life.

GOOD NEWS: By following these procedures and working on your goals every day, you will have several extra hours each week to pursue your own business, family and personal interests. Just remember, "When you do the things you need to do, when you need to do them, the day will come when you can do the things you want to do, when you want to do them."

MORE GOOD NEWS: When you learn the formula for setting one goal, you will know how to set all goals, whether it is a physical, mental, spiritual, social, family, career, recreational or financial goal.

NOW FOR THE ACTION STEPS:

Action Step 1

On your Dream List, let your imagination run wild and print everything you want to be, do or have. (When you **print**, your concentration is greater and you burn the idea more indelibly into your subconscious mind.) If you have a family, be sure to include your mate and children when you set your goals. This entire goal-setting process helps channel your logical left brain and frees your creative right brain for more effective use of your imagination.

NOTE: "You gotta '**be**' before you can '**do**,' and you gotta '**do**' before you can '**have**.'"

GO AHEAD—DO IT NOW. A major reason you are setting your goals is to gain some benefit, but these come only after you have taken action.

Action Step 2

Wait twenty-four to forty-eight hours then answer the question "why?" for each item you have printed on your Dream List. Space is provided for you to do this on your Things I Really Want To Be, Do or Have sheet. If you can't verbalize in one sentence why you want to "be, do or have," then it truly is a dream and not a real goal. At this point, you should cross it off your list.

Action Step 3

Ask these five questions, *all* of which must have a "yes" answer:

1. Is it really my goal? (If you're a minor living at home, an employee or a team member, some of your goals will be set by the coach, director, parent or employer.)

2. Is it morally right and fair to everyone concerned?

3. Is it consistent with my other goals?

4. Can I emotionally commit myself to finish this goal?

5. Can I "see" myself reaching this goal?

NOTE: Answering these questions will further reduce the number of dreams on your Things I Really Want To Be, Do or Have sheet, so scratch them off as well. Answering questions #2 and #3 will be very helpful in making important decisions in all areas of life, especially financial.

Action Step 4

After each remaining dream ask yourself these questions:

1. Will reaching this goal make me happier?

2. Will reaching this goal make me healthier?

3. Will reaching this goal make me more prosperous?
4. Will reaching this goal win me more friends?
5. Will reaching this goal give me peace of mind?
6. Will reaching this goal make me more secure?
7. Will reaching this goal improve my relationships with others?

If you can't answer "yes" to at least one of these questions eliminate that item from your list of dreams. Careful: Don't confuse pleasure with happiness. Be sure to consider your family when you answer these questions.

Action Step 5

Divide the remaining goals into three categories: Short range (1 month or less); Intermediate (1 month to 1 year); Long-range (1 year or more), and mark them SR (short range), I (intermediate) or LR (long-range) on your Things I Really Want To Be, Do or Have sheet. GO AHEAD—DO IT NOW. By taking this step you will be able to quickly determine whether or not you have a balanced perspective between what needs to be done now, versus your dreams for the future.

Remember:
1. SOME goals must be **big** (out of reach—not out of sight) to make you stretch and grow to your full potential.

2. SOME goals must be **long-range** to keep you on track and greatly reduce the possibility of short range frustrations.

3. SOME goals must be small and **daily** to keep you disciplined and in touch with the reality of "nitty gritties" of daily life.

4. SOME goals must be **ongoing**.

5. SOME goals (sales, educational, financial, weight loss, etc.) might require **analysis and consultation** to determine where you are before you can set the goals.

6. MOST goals should be **specific**. A "nice home" is not as good as "3,000 square foot, Tudor-style home with 4 bedrooms, 3 full baths, 2 living spaces," etc. Some goals, like improving your self-image, becoming a better parent or getting a better education, are more difficult to pinpoint. Those that are less specific should be broken down into specific, tangible steps. For instance, a step to becoming a better parent could be "spend one hour per week one-on-one with each child."

Action Step 6

From the remaining goals, prayerfully choose the four goals (remember, balance is the key) which are the most important things you need to work on right now and record them. If this is your first organized goal-setting experience, you may want to start with two or three short-range goals.

IMPORTANT: As you set a new goal, also record it in a journal or a place you will review several times a year. You will be encouraged tremendously as you record the goals you reach throughout the year. Your confidence, self-image and goals-achieving ability will improve dramatically.

Action Step 7

Record these four goals (at least the ones that are Intermediate and Long-Range) on a General Goals Procedure Chart, and work each one of them through the process as shown in the examples.

Action Step 8

Take the additional goals you have listed on your Things I Really Want To Be, Do or Have sheet and record each on a General Goals Procedure Chart. Work each goal through the process as you did in Action Step VII. Refer to the examples for a format to follow.

DO IT NOW. Remember, motivation comes **after** you start the project.

CONGRATULATIONS! You have invested more time in planning your future than most of your friends, relatives and associates will ever invest!

DREAM LIST
EVERYTHING—I even *think* I want to be, do or have

_____

_____

_____

_____

_____

_____

_____

_____

_____

_____

_____

_____

_____

_____

_____

_____

_____

_____

_____

Things I really want to be, do or have

After each item on your Dream List, articulate in one sentence why. This will eliminate those items which are frivolous whims but leave intact your serious goals and dreams.

Goals	Why

GENERAL GOALS PROCEDURE CHART

Step #1	IDENTIFY YOUR GOAL

Original Goal 165 lbs., 34" waist

Step #2	MY BENEFITS FOR REACHING THIS GOAL

More energy—less illness Look and feel better Longer life span Better endurance	More productivity Better attitude and disposition More creativity Better example

Step #3   MAJOR OBSTACLES AND MOUNTAINS
TO CLIMB TO REACH THIS GOAL

Lack of discipline Bad weather—irregular schedule Love for sweets—lack of time	Unhealthy eating habits Poor physical condition

Step #4   SKILLS OR KNOWLEDGE REQUIRED
TO REACH THIS GOAL

Dieting knowledge and techniques	Exercise and jogging procedures

Step #5   INDIVIDUALS, GROUPS, COMPANIES
AND ORGANIZATIONS TO WORK WITH
TO REACH THIS GOAL

Dr. Ken Cooper, Dr. Randy Martin, Program Chairman, Laurie Magers, The Redhead

Step #6	PLAN OF ACTION TO REACH THIS GOAL

Make commitment No bread or sweets except on Sunday Jog 125 minutes weekly Good breakfast—only fruit or healthy snacks after late seminars	Eat well-balanced diet Drink 8 glasses of water daily Eat slowly and only at the table

Step #7	COMPLETION DATE

July 1st

GENERAL GOALS PROCEDURE CHART

Step #1	IDENTIFY YOUR GOAL
Get a "Better" Education	

Step #2	MY BENEFITS FOR REACHING THIS GOAL

Broaden and increase opportunities
Improve self-image and increase
  relationships
Increase income
Improve security and knowledge
	Broaden personal, business and social
	  life and contacts
	Improve discipline—peace of mind
	Increase happiness—confidence
	Enhance sense of accomplishment

Step #3	MAJOR OBSTACLES AND MOUNTAINS TO CLIMB TO REACH THIS GOAL
Lack of patience—physical Exhaustion—financial costs	Heavy family demands—lack of confidence (out of school 15–20 yrs.)

Step #4	SKILLS OR KNOWLEDGE REQUIRED TO REACH THIS GOAL
Time management—positive attitude Patience—persistence—discipline	Better money management Effective study procedures

Step #5	INDIVIDUALS, GROUPS, COMPANIES AND ORGANIZATIONS TO WORK WITH TO REACH THIS GOAL
Family, Employer, Academic counselor, Financial consultant, Mentor	

Step #6	PLAN OF ACTION TO REACH THIS GOAL

Make commitment—organize time
Practice self-discipline (cut TV time)
Secure family support—schedule
  significant family time
Listen to educational, inspirational
  recordings while driving
	Attend seminars
	Reduce meaningless activities
	Schedule study time daily
	Shape up physically for increased energy

Step #7	COMPLETION DATE
None—on-going goal	

GENERAL GOALS PROCEDURE CHART

Step #1	IDENTIFY YOUR GOAL

Acquire a new black SUV with leather seats

Step #2	MY BENEFITS FOR REACHING THIS GOAL

More dependable transportation	Increase travel opportunities
Raise my sights and standards	Enhance social status
Improve job reliability	Greater safety
Better attitude	More comfort and fun

Step #3	MAJOR OBSTACLES AND MOUNTAINS TO CLIMB TO REACH THIS GOAL

Short of cash—Poor money management	Income stabilized—inflation—mate disagrees
Present car has low trade-in value	Higher payments and insurance costs

Step #4	SKILLS OR KNOWLEDGE REQUIRED TO REACH THIS GOAL

Money management—Automobile knowledge	Dollar stretching techniques
	Information on how to buy and trade

Step #5	INDIVIDUALS, GROUPS, COMPANIES AND ORGANIZATIONS TO WORK WITH TO REACH THIS GOAL

Family, Banker/Financier, Insurance agent, Employer, Investment counselor, Part-time employer, Automobile dealer

Step #6	PLAN OF ACTION TO REACH THIS GOAL

Get financial statement	Take family "window shopping" to see dream vehicle
Record expenditures for 30 days	
Skip vacation and deposit savings	Deposit savings every week in interest-bearing accounts
Follow ads and bargain hunt	
Establish and control budget	Take temporary and limited part-time job
Get family involved in their new vehicle	

Step #7	COMPLETION DATE

January 1st

GENERAL GOALS PROCEDURE CHART

Step #1 IDENTIFY YOUR GOAL	
Be a loving, attentive, involved parent	

Step #2 MY BENEFITS FOR REACHING THIS GOAL	
More happiness and peace of mind More stable marriage Better relationship with children, friends, neighbors and relatives	Better career opportunities More old age security Enjoyment of future grandchildren Increase potential of children

Step #3 MAJOR OBSTACLES AND MOUNTAINS TO CLIMB TO REACH THIS GOAL	
Limited experience—Tight budget Heavy workload—Lack of patience	Inadequate help or no help Alcoholic parent

Step #4 SKILLS OR KNOWLEDGE REQUIRED TO REACH THIS GOAL	

Mental, nutritional, spiritual and
  physical information
Discipline
Know something about being a "fixer"
	Read books on common sense,
	  diplomacy, communication skills, time
	  management, organizational skills

Step #5   INDIVIDUALS, GROUPS, COMPANIES AND ORGANIZATIONS TO WORK WITH TO REACH THIS GOAL
Minister, Employer, Family physician, Mate, Youth leaders, Educators, Parents,   In-laws, Neighbors, Parent support groups

Step #6 PLAN OF ACTION TO REACH THIS GOAL	

Read books on positive parenting methods
Assign daily responsibilities
Provide daily mental and spiritual input
  and direction
Spend time daily talking, directing,
  teaching and encouraging
Accept and love my kids unconditionally
	Give them daily doses of affection and
	  approval
	Expect, teach and require them to do
	  their best
	Discipline properly and consistently
	Admit when wrong and ask for
	  forgiveness

Step #7   COMPLETION DATE
Intangible

GENERAL GOALS PROCEDURE CHART

Step #1	IDENTIFY YOUR GOAL

Step #2	MY BENEFITS FOR REACHING THIS GOAL

Step #3	MAJOR OBSTACLES AND MOUNTAINS TO CLIMB TO REACH THIS GOAL

Step #4	SKILLS OR KNOWLEDGE REQUIRED TO REACH THIS GOAL

Step #5	INDIVIDUALS, GROUPS, COMPANIES AND ORGANIZATIONS TO WORK WITH TO REACH THIS GOAL

Step #6	PLAN OF ACTION TO REACH THIS GOAL

Step #7	COMPLETION DATE

Reaching Your Goals
(TO BE *CAREFULLY* READ AT THE END OF *EVERY WEEK*)

1. Make the commitment to reach your goal. "One person with a commitment is worth a hundred who only have an interest." —Mary Crowley

2. Commit yourself to detailed accountability. Record your weekly activities and list the six most important things, in the order of their importance, which you need to do tomorrow. Daily discipline is the **key** to reaching your goals.

3. Build your life on a solid foundation of honesty, character, faith, integrity, love and loyalty. This foundation will give you an honest shot at reaching any goal you have properly set.

4. Break your Intermediate and Long-Range goals into increments. Examples: I lost 37 pounds by losing 3.7 pounds each month for 10 months, or just 1.9 ounces per day. I wrote *See You at the Top* (348 pages) by writing 1.26 pages per day, every day, for 10 months. (By the mile it's a trial, by the inch it's a cinch!)

5. Shape up mentally, physically and spiritually. It takes energy, mental toughness and spiritual

reinforcement to successfully deal with life's op-
portunities, and to reach your objectives.

    A. Motivation is the key and a positive attitude
is a must, so on a daily basis you should feed
your mind with good, clean, pure, powerful and positive material by reading good
books and listening to motivational, educational and inspirational recordings. Regularly attend personal growth seminars
or industry related training lectures and
training programs. Remember, what you
do off the job is going to be a determining
factor in how far you go on the job.

    B. Take care of your physical health—proper
diet, reasonable sleep, exercise, and eliminate the poisons (alcohol, drugs and tobacco).

    C. Don't let others rain on your parade—or
don't be a SNIOP (**S**usceptible to the **N**ega-
tive **I**nfluence of **O**ther **P**eople).

6. Be prepared to change. You can't control the
weather, inflation, interest rates, Wall Street,
etc. Just remember that, at this point, your goals
have been **carefully** (and, I hope, prayerfully)
set, so change your decision to go, carefully, but
be willing to change your direction to get there
as conditions and circumstances demand.

7. Share your "give-up" goals (give up smoking,
being rude, procrastination, being late, eating

too much, etc.) with many people. Chances are excellent they are going to encourage you. Share your "go up" goals (be #1 producer, write a book, graduate with honors and be the class valedictorian, etc.) only with those rare people you strongly feel will give you support and encouragement.

8. Become a team player. Learn to work with a team, such as your family, corporate associates, etc. Remember, "You can have everything in life you want if you will just help enough other people get what they want."

9. See the reaching. In your imagination, see yourself receiving that diploma, getting that job or promotion, making that speech, moving into the home of your dreams, achieving that weight loss goal, building that financial nest egg, etc.

10. Each time you reach a goal, your confidence will grow that you can do bigger and better things. After accomplishing the goal, record the event and cross it off your Things I Really Want to Be, Do or Have sheet.

CRITICAL: Immediately set a new goal and work that new goal through the General Goals Procedure Chart.

11. Remember that what you **get** by reaching your destination is not nearly so important as what you will become by reaching your goals, because what you will **become** is the **winner** you were born to be.

NOTE: Since motivation is critical in the goal-setting and goal-achieving process, it would be helpful if you had our series on goals or our complete "How To Stay Motivated" series.

CPSIA information can be obtained
at www.ICGtesting.com
Printed in the USA
JSHW011909300423
40998JS00006B/6